AF422841

Ride For Your Brand: A Small-Town Story of Faith, Family, and Starting Over

By Steven R. Wiatrek

Ride For Your Brand: A Small-Town Story of Faith, Family, and
Starting Over
© 2026 Steven R.. Wiatrek

All rights reserved. No part of this publication may be reproduced,
distributed, or transmitted in any form or by any means, including
photocopying, recording, or other electronic or mechanical methods,
without the prior written permission of the author, except in the case
of brief quotations embodied in critical reviews and certain other
noncommercial uses permitted by copyright law.

ISBN: 979-8-9949192-0-0

Published by:
Wiatrek Group LLC
Poth, Texas, USA

This book represents the personal opinions, experiences, and
observations of the author. It is not intended as legal, financial, or
professional advice. The views expressed are solely those of the author
and do not reflect those of any past, present, or future employer,
business partner, or affiliate.

Printed in the United States of America
First Edition – 2026

DEDICATION

To my family—
the living, the remembered, and the generations yet to come.
You are the soil in which my roots were planted,
the shelter that held me through my darkest seasons,
and the quiet strength that pushed me forward
when the world tried to convince me I had nothing left to give.
Every chapter of this book exists because of you.

"There is within you something that waits and listens for the sound of the genuine in yourself."
— Howard Thurman

AUTHOR'S NOTE

This book was born from a quieter place than my first.
The Not-So-Secret Guide to Insurance Sales was written from
momentum—from the fire of rebuilding, from the fierce
determination of a man who had walked through the storm and
decided to raise his flag again.
But this book—Ride for Your Brand—came from somewhere deeper.
Book One told people how I rebuilt my life.
Book Two tells them why I had to.

x

TABLE OF CONTENTS

Introduction

Introduction

There comes a moment in every man's life when he must sit still long enough to listen to the quiet voice inside—the one he ignores when life is loud, when business is busy, and when the world demands one more task, one more sale, one more moment of his attention.

Most men never pause long enough to hear it.

But life has a way of slowing a man down when he refuses to slow himself. And when that day comes—when the noise finally settles—a man faces something far more confronting than failure or hardship.

He faces himself.

I never set out to write this book. Truthfully, I never believed I would write even one. I was a small-town insurance agent from South Texas—a husband, a father, a man doing his best to build a life of meaning for the people he loved most.

But life has a remarkable way of reshaping our plans and forcing us onto roads we never intended to walk.

This book was born out of such a season—a season that tested me in ways I did not see coming, a season that stripped away titles, certainty, and comfort, and left me alone with questions I could no longer outrun.

Who am I when the role disappears? What do I stand for when the structure collapses? And does my voice still matter when the applause fades?

It took losing a title to discover the strength of my character. It took walking away from a company to understand who I was without a logo behind me. And it took starting over to realize my value had never been determined by someone else's opinion.

Some lessons arrive gently. The most enduring ones rarely do.

In the quiet aftermath of that season, I found myself driving the back roads of South Texas—long stretches of earth and sky where a man has room to think.

There is something sacred about those roads—the kind of sacred found only in places where honesty still matters and a man's word still carries weight.

Those miles reminded me where I came from. They reminded me of the values planted in me long before I had language for them.

Part I – Breaking Point

At the bottom of the mountain, you remember who you really are.
-   C.S. Lewis

Chapter 1: The Day Everything Changed

I remember it with a clarity that still catches me off guard—the day I walked away from the captive insurance world, the company and office I had been part of for more than a decade.
Ten and a half years of routines had trained my body to move before my mind was fully awake. I parked in the same oil slicked spot I always had, stepped out of my truck, and paused for just a moment before walking inside. The December air was sharp, clean, and cold enough to wake a man up. Christmas decorations lined the street, cheerful and confident, as if the world had already decided everything was going to be fine.
Inside the office, the lights hummed softly. The smell of stale coffee lingered in the air. Desks sat neatly arranged, calendars still turned to December, unfinished tasks frozen in time. The Christmas wreath on the front door felt out of place—too festive for the weight pressing against my chest.
I sat down at my desk and rested my hands on the worn surface I knew so well. This desk had seen late nights and early mornings, hard conversations and quiet victories. It had held policy files, handwritten notes, and more than a few moments of silent prayer. For years, it had felt like a place of purpose.

That morning, it felt like borrowed ground. The realization hit me harder than I expected. My head went light. My breathing turned shallow. That hollow sensation crept into my legs—the kind that warns a man his world is about to tilt before his mind has time to catch up.

And one thought cut through everything else:

What am I going to do now?

My wife was a stay-at-home mother. We had three young children depending on me. And it was December 23rd—the office closing early for Christmas, and my career closing with it.

The truth was, none of this should have surprised me.

Painful? Yes. Unexpected? No.

I had been walking toward this edge for months, even as I convinced myself the ground would somehow hold.

Six months earlier, upper management had called me in. The meeting was calm, polished, rehearsed—the kind of conversation that pretends to be supportive while quietly delivering a verdict.

"You're behind on your life insurance quotas," they said. "This is the second year you'll miss them."

I listened carefully, choosing my words the way a man does when he knows every syllable might be used against him.

Then came the line that cut deeper than they realized.

"You were once a top performer. Then COVID happened, and you never bounced back."

They warned me plainly: hit the numbers or face consequences.

I swallowed the sting, squared my shoulders, and told them I would do my best. I meant it. Every word.

But something had already cracked.

I walked back to my office, closed the door, and sat down. The room felt smaller than it ever had. The walls that once felt protective now felt confining.

It didn't feel like a place of opportunity anymore.

It felt like a cage.

Tears came without permission—hot, frustrated, unwelcome.

A few minutes later, there was a soft knock at the door.

My manager stepped inside and closed it behind him. He pulled a chair up slowly and sat across from me.

"Steven," he said quietly, "I'm sorry. Truly."

It's admirable that you want to make one last push, he told me. But the odds are stacked against you now. And the pressure is going to eat you alive.

He wasn't threatening me. He was warning me.

The months that followed were the hardest of my career.

Agent of the Month. Runner-up. Trips. Recognition.

Each award felt like a cup of water thrown on a house fire.

Rates climbed. Rules tightened. The math refused to bend.

On November 1st, I stared at the numbers.

Impossible.

They offered me two options.

Resign. Or have my contract pulled.

If leaving was inevitable, then I would leave standing.

December 23rd arrived faster than I was ready for.

I packed my books. Then the photographs. Then the plaques.

I wasn't just packing an office. I was burying a season of my life.

The drive home was short, but it felt endless.

That night, staring at the ceiling, the truth surfaced.

I had walked away from a version of myself that could no longer carry the life I was meant to build.

This was not my ending.

This was the beginning of my becoming.

Chapter 2: Losing the Title, Keeping the Man

The morning after I walked out of that office, the world felt unfamiliar—not because anything around me had changed, but because I had.

The house was quiet in a way I wasn't used to. Not peaceful. Not calm. Just empty. The kind of silence that presses against a man's chest and dares him to fill it with answers he doesn't yet have. There was no alarm clock demanding movement, no calendar dictating purpose, no role waiting to be filled.

For the first time in more than ten years, there was nowhere I needed to be.

No office to unlock. No numbers to chase. No title to carry into the day.

I sat on the edge of the bed longer than I should have, staring at the floor as if it might tell me what came next. My hands rested on my knees, motionless, useless. My chest felt tight, as though my body was bracing for a blow that never quite landed.

I wasn't tired.

I was untethered.

When I finally walked into the kitchen, my wife looked up from the counter and studied my face. She didn't rush toward me or ask questions. She simply watched—the way someone does when they sense something has shifted but don't yet know how deep it goes.

My children were already at the table, pancakes half-eaten, laughter spilling louder than the mess they were making. Syrup clung to their fingers. Milk had splashed across the table. Life, to them, was still uncomplicated.

One of them knocked over the bottle of syrup, and it spread across the table in slow amber lines, dripping onto the floor while they laughed and reached for paper towels they couldn't quite manage. Pancakes. Syrup. Sticky fingers. Life moving forward in its small, unbothered way.

I stood there watching it happen, struck by how the world doesn't pause when a man loses his footing. Children still laugh. Breakfast still gets made. Messes still need cleaning—even when a man's identity feels like it's just been ripped away.

I forced a smile. Forced normal. Forced a strength I didn't yet feel.

Inside, something was unraveling.

Later that morning, I stepped outside because the walls felt too close. The winter air cut sharp against my lungs, honest and unforgiving. I crossed the yard and rested my hand against the bare crepe myrtle, its branches reaching upward, stripped of everything but still standing.

It looked exactly how I felt.

For years, my identity had been clear. Producer. Leader. Provider. The man people called when they needed answers. The man with a desk, a territory, and a place to belong.

Now I was none of those things.

I was just a man standing in his yard, unemployed, unsure, and quietly terrified of what that meant for the people who depended on me.

My phone buzzed in my pocket.

Are you okay? What happened? Did you quit? Call me.

I didn't answer.

Not because I didn't care—but because I didn't yet have words that didn't feel like excuses.

The applications started soon after.

At first, they felt hopeful. Then practical. Then desperate.

Ten turned into fifty. Fifty into a hundred. A hundred into more than two hundred.

Each one felt less like a step forward and more like asking permission to exist. Every rejection chipped away at a place inside me that was already raw.

Some companies told me I was overqualified. Others said I was too expensive. Most said nothing at all.

Silence became its own verdict.

A few days later, I ran into someone I knew at the grocery store.

He smiled when he saw me, confident and relaxed, the way people are when they believe they know where you belong in the world.

"Hey, Steven," he said. "How's the office?"

The question caught me off guard—not because it was rude, but because it was automatic. A reflex. My name had always come with a title attached to it, and without it, I felt strangely incomplete answering.

"I'm not there anymore," I said.

There was a pause. Not long. Just long enough.

His smile faltered for a fraction of a second before he recovered.

"Oh," he said. "Well… what are you doing now?"

I didn't know how to answer that.

"I'm figuring it out," I said finally.

He nodded politely, the way people do when a conversation has reached its natural end. We exchanged a few more harmless words, and then he moved on.

I stood there longer than necessary, staring at a shelf of canned goods I didn't need, feeling something settle heavy in my chest.

That's when it hit me:

The world hadn't changed how it saw me.

It had simply stopped seeing me.

Without a title, without a role that explained my worth in a single sentence, I had become invisible in a way I'd never experienced before.

It wasn't cruelty. It wasn't judgment.

It was indifference.

And indifference cuts deeper than rejection.

I noticed it again at church. Conversations that once lingered now ended quickly. Questions that used to come easily were replaced with polite nods. No one meant harm—but no one knew where to place me anymore.

For years, I had believed respect was built on character.

In that season, I learned how much of it had been built on position.

And that realization hurt more than losing the job itself.

At night, when the house finally went still and distractions faded, the thoughts came louder.

You failed your family. You should have seen this coming. You were never as secure as you thought.

I prayed—but not with polished words. These were clenched-teeth prayers. Desperate ones whispered into the dark.

My wife tried to stay strong. I could see it in her posture, the way she held herself just a little tighter. Fear leaked through no matter how carefully we tried to contain it.

Bitterness followed close behind—toward the company, toward the system, toward myself for believing loyalty would always be enough.

Rock bottom has a way of stripping a man bare.

When the title disappears, when the applause fades, when the structure collapses, there is nowhere left to hide.

One cold night, after another day of unanswered applications and prayers that felt like they bounced off the ceiling, I stepped back outside.

The neighborhood was silent. Streetlights cast long shadows across the yard.

The crepe myrtle stood motionless against the night sky.

And then, slowly, something shifted.

Not hope. Not confidence. Not certainty.

Acceptance.

I had lost the title.
But I had not lost the man.
And that truth stayed.
Because the man who survives the stripping is the man capable of rebuilding.
And whatever came next would be built on something deeper—something no one could take away.

Chapter 3: When Three Doors Appeared

The strange thing about hitting bottom is that nothing changes all at once.

There was no moment when the fear disappeared or the uncertainty lifted. No sudden clarity. No dramatic breakthrough. Life didn't snap back into place just because I had accepted where I stood. The days still arrived quietly, one after another, asking to be lived even when I wasn't sure how.

What changed was quieter than that.

I stopped running from the question of what came next—and started listening for answers. After weeks of silence, rejection, and prayer that felt unanswered, three opportunities began to surface. Not all at once. Not with certainty. But enough to remind me that my story wasn't finished.

They didn't feel like answers.

They felt like doors.

And between those doors was a space far heavier than I expected— the waiting.

There were days when I deliberately did nothing.

Not because I was avoiding responsibility, but because I was trying to hear clearly. I took longer walks. I drove back roads without music. I

let the discomfort sit without rushing to fix it. I learned quickly that
indecision has its own weight, and that delaying a choice doesn't
relieve pressure—it concentrates it.
Every day without a decision still cost something.
Peace. Sleep. Confidence.
Not choosing yet was still choosing.

The first door was familiar.
It came in the form of another captive insurance company—different
logo, same structure. Predictable income. Clear expectations. A path
back to stability.
On paper, it made sense.
The conversations were professional. The language was reassuring.
They spoke about culture, growth, and opportunity in the same
polished tone I had heard before. The benefits were easy to list. The
path was already drawn.
Too familiar.
As I listened, I could already feel the weight returning—the quotas, the
pressure, the quiet erosion of autonomy disguised as support. I could
picture the late nights justified by numbers, the compromises
explained away as temporary, the constant awareness that someone
else always held the final say.
It wasn't fear holding me back.
It was recognition.
I knew where that road led.
That door would give me stability—but it would also cost me
ownership. It would bring a paycheck home, but it would bring the
same tension with it. My family would feel it even if they never saw it
written on a contract.
That door offered comfort.
At a price I had already paid once.

The second door came from a different direction.
A non-insurance role. Leadership-based. Sales-adjacent. A chance to apply my experience without carrying the same pressure.
It promised balance.
Fewer nights on edge. Fewer weekends interrupted. A quieter version of life.
And for a moment, I wanted it.
I imagined dinners without distraction. Holidays without dread. A life where success didn't demand constant vigilance. A version of myself that could finally exhale.
But the longer I sat with it, the clearer something became.
That door didn't scare me.
And that worried me.
It felt like stepping aside instead of stepping forward. Like choosing relief over responsibility. It wasn't wrong. It was respectable. It made sense to nearly everyone I described it to.
But it didn't ask much of me.
And I knew—quietly, uncomfortably—that the man I wanted to be couldn't grow inside something that required less of him than he was capable of giving.
That door offered ease.
At the cost of calling.

The third door didn't arrive the way opportunities usually do.
It didn't begin with a pitch or a promise. It started as a conversation between two insurance professionals—nothing more.
Neil had reached out to me through LinkedIn. We had never spoken before. When we connected, there was no shop talk, no posturing, no attempt to impress. We talked about the industry the way people do when they've both been in it long enough to know what matters and what doesn't.
No selling. No positioning. Just conversation.

Near the end of that first call, calmly and politely, Neil asked a single question:

"Would you be open to talking about an agency ownership opportunity?"

There was no pressure in how he asked it. No urgency. No framing it as something I needed to decide on the spot.

I told him the truth.

"I'd need to sleep on it and talk to my wife."

He didn't push. He didn't counter. He respected it.

That alone stood out.

That night, my wife and I talked longer than usual. Not about projections or promises—but about life. About what we had just lived through. About the weight that had followed me home for years without either of us naming it.

We talked about our children. About the kind of household we wanted them to grow up in. About the example we were setting—not with words, but with choices.

By the time we went to bed, the decision was clear.

Not to say yes.

But to learn.

The next morning, I signed the NDA.

Only then did the real conversation begin.

With confidentiality in place, Neil laid everything out—openly and without insulation. There was no sugarcoating. No fluff. No attempt to dress the opportunity up as something it wasn't.

What you saw was what you got.

We talked through the realities: the risk, the responsibility, the learning curve, the weight of ownership. He didn't promise safety or certainty. He didn't pretend independence was easy.

If it worked, it would be because I built it. If it failed, there would be no one else to blame.

At one point, he said something simply, without emphasis:

"You won't answer to a quota anymore—but you'll answer to yourself every day."
There was no drama in how he said it. Just fact.
And that mattered.

I spent days sitting with all three doors in front of me.
I compared them not by benefits, but by cost.
One would cost autonomy. One would cost growth. One would cost certainty.
Every door charged a price.
The question wasn't which one paid more.
It was which one I was willing to live with.
I didn't announce the decision when it finally settled in me.
There was no relief. No celebration. No sense of victory.
Just a quiet resolve that arrived without witnesses.
I understood then that the most important decisions a man makes are rarely loud. They aren't posted. They aren't applauded.
They are carried.
I didn't walk through that door with confidence.
I walked through it with resolve.
And for the first time since everything had fallen apart, that felt like enough.

Part II – Finding My Voice Again

Do not Judge me by my success, judge me by how many times I fell down and got back up again.
                    Nelson Mandela

Chapter 4: Stepping Into the Unknown

By February, the ashes of my old life had finally settled.
The decision had been made. The ships had been burned.
But the truth—the kind you only admit when no one is listening—was that the weight of stepping into a brand-new world, alone, unproven, and untested, was only beginning to press down on my shoulders.
There is a silence that follows a life-altering decision.
Not peace.
Not relief.
But a heavy, echoing quiet that presses against your chest and whispers, "It's all on you now."
I used to think the hard part was walking out. I used to think the hard part was losing the office, the title, the routine. But once the dust settled, I realized the real weight wasn't the loss—it was the responsibility that came after it. Loss is something that happens to you. Responsibility is something you choose to carry.
Ambition burned inside me like a torch, but doubt followed close behind, clinging like a shadow that refused to let go. I had chosen a path that offered no guarantees, no safety net, and no one to blame if it failed. For the first time in my professional life, the responsibility was absolute.

And the people who loved me most could feel it too.

Even the small things felt heavier. The way I looked at the calendar. The way I checked my bank account. The way I lingered in the doorway before walking into the house, as if I could leave the pressure outside if I paused long enough.

But pressure doesn't stay on the porch.

Family Fear — A Battle on the Homefront

My family supported me—genuinely and deeply.

But fear lived behind their eyes, and fear has a way of slipping quietly into everyday conversations. It shows up in tone. In pauses. In the questions that don't need answers but still need to be asked.

They had never heard of an insurance distribution firm. To them, it didn't sound like innovation. It sounded like a trap.

A gamble.

A risk.

A chance to lose everything we had worked for.

"You're going to get taken for a ride."

"This sounds too good to be true."

"You're risking everything."

"What if this doesn't work?"

"Why leave stability?"

They weren't doubting my ability.

They were terrified of another fall.

They had watched me climb for more than a decade. They had watched me pour myself into my work, sacrifice evenings, weekends, and peace of mind to provide for the people I loved. And then they had watched it all collapse in a single day.

They didn't want to see the man of the house—the protector, the provider—fall again.

Their fear wasn't a lack of faith.

It was love, wearing the only armor it knew how to wear.

And the hard part wasn't hearing their worry—it was feeling how reasonable it sounded. I could understand every question. I could hear the logic in it. And sometimes, if I'm being honest, I wanted to borrow their fear because it felt like a permission slip to step back into something predictable.

But I couldn't unlearn what I had learned.

The old life had required me to swallow too much. To accept pressure as normal. To call anxiety "drive." To mistake exhaustion for excellence. And I couldn't ask my family to live inside that again just because it came with the appearance of stability.

One evening, after the kids had finally settled down and the house had gone quiet, my wife and I sat at the table longer than usual. The kitchen light was the only one on. The rest of the house felt dark and still, like it was listening.

She didn't raise her voice. She didn't accuse. She just asked the question that mattered most:

"Do you believe this is the right thing?"

I didn't answer quickly. Not because I didn't know—but because I wanted the answer to be honest, not brave.

"I do," I said. "But I'm scared too."

That admission changed something between us. Not because it fixed the fear, but because it named it. For so long, I had carried pressure like it was my private duty, like speaking it aloud would make me weaker. In that season, I learned that real strength isn't pretending you aren't afraid.

Real strength is carrying the fear and moving forward anyway— without lying to the people you love.

And while their words stirred doubt, they also forced me to confront a deeper truth: the safe road no longer existed. The old life was gone. Stability, as I once understood it, had already been taken from me.

This uncertain path wasn't reckless.

It was the only one that aligned with the man I was becoming.

Small-Town Echoes

In a small Texas town, news travels faster than the wind.
Everywhere I went—the grocery store, the feed store, the gas station, church—someone stopped me. There was no anonymity, no quiet place to process what had happened. If you're hurting in a small town, you hurt in public. If you're rebuilding, everyone can see the lumber.
Some apologized.
"Steven, you deserved better than what they did to you."
Some vented.
"Service hasn't been the same since you left. It's gone downhill."
But most offered something that shook me to my core.
"Wherever you land, we're following you."
Those words carried weight. Loyalty always does.
Because loyalty isn't a compliment. It's a responsibility.
It meant people were watching how I handled the fall. Watching whether I became bitter, whether I disappeared, whether I turned my pain into poison. In a small town, your reputation isn't your marketing—it's your history.
Then came the moment that humbled me more than any praise ever could.
A longtime client pulled me aside, lowered his voice, and said, "Steven, I don't care what it costs. I'll pay thousands more a year if it means you can be my agent again."
I shook my head immediately.
Not because I wasn't grateful—but because I knew what that kind of loyalty can tempt a man to do. It can tempt you to take shortcuts. To leverage trust unfairly. To let emotion override wisdom.
And I refused.
Because what mattered wasn't winning business—it was earning trust the right way. That moment reminded me that relationships built over years don't disappear with a title. They wait. They watch. And they remember how you treated people when no one was keeping score.

What moved me most was not the money he mentioned. It was the
sentence beneath the sentence:
You mattered here.
Not as a producer.
Not as a number.
As a man.

The Unknown Doesn't Ask Permission

The days that followed were a strange mixture of motion and stillness. I was working, but it didn't feel like the old work. There were no quotas yelling from a spreadsheet. No daily meetings. No corporate voice reminding me what mattered.

That freedom was real—but it was also heavier than I expected.

Some mornings I woke up with energy, ready to build. Other mornings I woke up with a dull uncertainty that lingered like fog. On those days, I had to remind myself that doubt doesn't mean you chose wrong. It means you're human.

At night, when the house finally grew quiet, doubt returned.

Not loudly.

Not dramatically.

Just enough to make sleep harder to find.

I lay awake wondering if patience would eventually pay off or if I was mistaking conviction for stubbornness. Whether discipline would turn into momentum or simply become another lesson learned the hard way. Whether I was building a future or just chasing a hope.

Those were not comfortable questions.

But they were honest ones.

And honesty became the new foundation.

I prayed differently in that season. Less like a man trying to impress God with the right words, and more like a man telling the truth.

Sometimes it was a full prayer. Sometimes it was just a sentence whispered into the dark:

"Lord, don't let me ruin what I'm trying to build."

Sometimes it was quieter than that—just a breath, just a plea, just a willingness to keep going.

And slowly, I noticed something.

The doubts no longer felt like verdicts.

They felt like part of the cost.

Every meaningful path demands something in return.

The question wasn't whether I would pay a price.
The question was whether the price was worth what I was building.

Stepping into the unknown wasn't brave.
It was necessary.
I hadn't chosen certainty. I had chosen integrity.
I hadn't chosen comfort. I had chosen alignment.
I hadn't chosen the easiest road. I had chosen the one that matched my conscience.
And slowly—quietly—I began to understand that rebuilding a life isn't about moving fast.
It's about moving true.
One honest conversation.
One disciplined day.
One decision made with my family in mind.
One step forward without pretending the fear isn't there.
That's how the rebuild began.
Not with applause.
With resolve.

I didn't need the unknown to feel comfortable. I just needed it to be honest.
Because if I could build on honesty—on real service, real relationships, and the kind of work that lets a man sleep at night—then the future didn't have to be guaranteed to be worth pursuing.
It only had to be true.

Chapter 5: The Brotherhood I Didn't Know I Needed

As February turned into March, the rhythm of independence began to settle into my bones.

I was still stumbling, still doubting myself, still wrestling with the ghosts of my past—but something else was happening too. Independence didn't bring instant clarity. It brought exposure. Without a system to lean on, every weakness became visible. Every habit was tested. Every motive was stripped bare.

There were mornings I questioned whether I had traded certainty for chaos. Nights where the quiet felt louder than any meeting room ever had. Independence forces a man to confront himself, not as he wishes to be seen, but as he truly is.

Yet beneath that discomfort, something deeper stirred.

The fire inside me—the one I thought had died somewhere between quotas, pressure, and quiet disappointment—was beginning to burn again. Not recklessly. Not loudly. But steadily. Purposefully. Like a flame that had survived the storm and was finally being fed oxygen.

When the announcement came for the next Agency Owner meeting in Houston, I registered immediately.

This wasn't just another meeting. This was my chance to see the culture up close, to meet the leaders, to stand in the room where my new future was being shaped. After months of uncertainty, I needed confirmation—not of success, but of alignment.
I didn't know it yet, but this meeting would become one of the defining moments of my entire journey.

Arriving Early — Four Hours on the Road, and Still One Hour Ahead
The meeting was set for 10:00 a.m. Houston was four hours away. Most people would've left at six. Most would've planned to slide in right on time, blending into the room unnoticed.
Not me.
I left long before sunrise, the highway stretching before me like a ribbon of possibility. The world was quiet. The sky was dark. And for the first time in months, my thoughts weren't anxious or spiraling. They were hopeful.
The hum of the road gave me time to think—not the painful thoughts that had haunted me earlier in the year, but thoughts of renewal. Of rebirth. Of what life could look like if integrity came before approval.
I thought about the man I had been, the man I was becoming, and the man my family needed me to be. I wasn't chasing applause anymore. I was chasing peace.
When I pulled into the parking lot at 9:00 a.m., an hour early even after a four-hour drive, I stepped out of my truck wearing my suit and carrying my briefcase like a man reporting for his destiny.
Leadership noticed.
"You know you're early, right?" one of them said with a grin.
"Yes, sir," I replied. "But if you're on time… you're late."
He laughed—but it wasn't patronizing. It was respect. Recognition. A quiet acknowledgment of values that don't need explanation.
Before the day even began, I felt something shift.

This place sees me. This place gets me. This place respects how I operate.

Meeting the Other Agency Owners — Finding My People
As other owners began to arrive, the room filled with an energy you can't manufacture.
These were men and women who had lived a thousand versions of my story. Different companies. Different cities. Different timelines.
But the same bruises. The same battles. The same scars.
One by one, they shook my hand. They shared their experiences openly—pressure from the captive world, fear of starting over, the relief of finally building something honest.
There was no bravado in the room. No pretending. Just truth spoken freely among people who had earned it.
For the first time in months, I didn't feel like a man starting from zero.
I felt seen. Understood. Accepted.
These weren't strangers.
These were my people.
People who had hurt like I had. People who had walked through the same fire. People who had chosen not to die in the ashes.
And in their stories, I heard pieces of my own. Their failures mirrored mine. Their courage reminded me of what was still possible.
Belonging settled in quietly, but firmly.

A Leader Unlike Any I Had Ever Seen
Then a man walked into the room wearing a suit and a smile that filled the space.
He shook hands with everyone. He laughed easily. He listened carefully. He spoke to each agent like an equal—not a subordinate.
At first, I assumed he was a senior agency owner.
Then someone leaned over and whispered, "That's Jody. The CEO."
I froze.

Because in more than a decade at my previous company, I had never
seen leadership act that way. I had seen authority, control, hierarchy—
but not humility.

This wasn't authority through distance.

This was leadership through presence.

And before he ever stepped on stage, he earned my respect.

This was the kind of leadership that didn't demand loyalty—it inspired
it.

The Words That Changed Everything

When the meeting began, Jody stepped forward and said something that shook me to my core.

"Let's make one thing clear," he said. "We are not family."

The room went silent.

Then he continued.

"Family doesn't always treat each other right. We don't choose our family.

But partnership? Partnership is chosen.

We choose to ride together. We choose to give 100% to one another—not because we have to, but because we want to."

In that moment, the fog lifted.

This wasn't a company hiding behind clichés. This wasn't corporate polish. This was truth.

It was a standard. A boundary. An invitation to mutual respect.

And sitting there, surrounded by men and women cut from the same cloth, I knew:

I made the right choice.

The Drive Home — Freedom I Could Feel in My Bones

When the meeting ended and I walked back to my truck, something inside me felt reborn.

Not instantly—but undeniably.

As Houston faded in the rearview mirror, a smile spread across my face.

Not a mask. Not a performance. But real joy.

I rolled down the window. Let the wind rush in. The invisible chains I'd carried for years—pressure, quotas, fear—fell away.

And with them, the depression that had hollowed me out finally lifted.

Despite having no money, no clients, and no guarantees, I felt something stronger than certainty.

I felt purpose.

As the miles rolled beneath my tires, I whispered three words into the open road:

"I'm going to make it."

And for the first time since losing everything, I believed it.

Night settled over the Texas sky as I pulled into my driveway. The road ahead was uncertain—but I wasn't afraid.

Because men aren't defined by the roads they travel.

They're defined by the roads they choose.

And I knew this was the road I was meant to walk.

What stayed with me most from that day wasn't a speech or a statistic. It was the absence of fear in the room. No one was guarding their position. No one was posturing. The success of one didn't threaten the success of another.

That was new to me.

For years, I had been conditioned to believe that leadership meant distance and that success required competition. But in that room, I saw something healthier—men and women who understood that shared values create stronger results than shared fear ever could.

Driving those long miles home, I realized something else: I wasn't rebuilding alone.

The word brotherhood took on a new meaning. It wasn't about blood or obligation. It was about shared responsibility. Shared standards. Shared resolve.

I hadn't just found a business model.

I had found people who would walk with me.

And that realization changed everything.

I thought about how different that felt from everything I had known before. In the past, success had always felt conditional. Temporary. Something that could be taken the moment you slowed down or questioned the system. It created a constant low-grade anxiety that never fully left.

But what I felt now was steadier.

This brotherhood wasn't built on production numbers alone. It was built on character. On showing up prepared. On keeping your word. On treating people with dignity whether they were buying something or not.

That realization reshaped how I viewed the road ahead.

I wasn't chasing freedom just for myself anymore. I was building something that could last—something my family could be proud of, something rooted in service rather than pressure.

As I shut off the engine and sat in the driveway for a moment longer than usual, I understood something clearly:

This wasn't an ending.

It was alignment.

And for the first time in a very long time, that felt like more than enough.

Because when a man finally finds where he belongs, the work ahead no longer feels heavy. It feels meaningful.

And that difference makes all the difference in the world.

The road ahead was still long, but I no longer questioned whether it was worth walking.

I had found my footing, and with it, my confidence.

That night, I slept without fear for the first time in months.

And that alone was a victory.

A real one.

Chapter 6: Building the Foundation

The weeks after my Houston meeting felt different—not just on the surface, but deep inside my spirit.

Something inside me had shifted, awakened, healed. For the first time since leaving my old company, I didn't feel like a man clawing his way out of the ashes.

I felt like a man preparing to build.

But building something meaningful is never glamorous in the beginning.

It doesn't start with applause or recognition. It doesn't begin with momentum or money. It begins in silence—with long days, quiet nights, and unseen battles fought behind closed doors.

That was the season I had entered.

The Quiet Work No One Sees

March became a month of relentless, uncelebrated work.

No cheering crowds. No incoming revenue. No scoreboard. No quotas. No pressure from above.

Just me—choosing to rise, choosing to learn, choosing to build.

My old life had been governed by quotas and fear. This life? It was governed by opportunity—and what I chose to do with it.

Our firm didn't monitor me. No one counted my calls. No one demanded production deadlines. No one hovered over me waiting to punish mistakes.

For the first time in my entire career, my success depended entirely on my effort—not someone else's expectations.

And that freedom made me hungrier than fear ever did.

I spent hours learning new systems, studying carrier appetites, memorizing guidelines, and correcting my own mistakes. Some days were discouraging. Some days I wondered if progress was even happening at all.

But every small breakthrough—every system I finally understood, every process that clicked—reminded me of something important: This is mine. This foundation is mine. This future is mine.

Learning the Independent World

Transitioning from captive to independent was like learning a new language—one spoken by builders instead of followers.

There was no IT department waiting to rescue me. No standardized scripts. No safety rails.

If something broke, I fixed it. If something confused me, I studied it. If something failed, I owned it.

Some days I stared at my computer with frustration boiling just beneath the surface.

"What if you can't do this?" "What if you weren't meant for this world?" "What if you're pretending to be stronger than you are?" Those questions came often.

But this time, doubt wasn't the only voice in the room.

Pride—quiet, steady pride—began to rise. Not pride in results. Not pride in numbers. But pride in effort.

Pride in discipline. Pride in showing up. Pride in refusing to quit.

I was no longer an agent begging to be valued.

I was a business owner building something of my own.

And that realization changed everything.

Small Sparks of Momentum
Slowly, almost silently, momentum began to form.
I completed my first accurate independent quotes. I navigated systems without panic. Carrier representatives sent encouragement. Other agency owners offered advice freely. My confidence returned piece by piece. My skill level improved week after week.
None of it made headlines.
But it mattered.
Then something unexpected started happening.
Agents began reaching out to me.
Not because I was outperforming anyone. Not because leadership spotlighted me. Not because I was the most experienced.
But because my work ethic was visible.
They saw my hunger. My consistency. My willingness to grind quietly.
Before long, my phone rang with questions:
"Steven, how are you organizing your workflow?" "How did you learn these carriers so fast?" "Can you help me understand this underwriting guideline?"
Me—the man who had been unemployed only weeks earlier.
It humbled me. But it also revealed a truth I would never forget:
Leadership isn't a title. Leadership is influence—earned through effort.

Adding My First Producer — And the Promise I Made to Myself
Then came one of the most defining moments of my early journey.
A young man reached out. Licensed. Hungry. Determined. Willing to invest in himself.
But the captive world didn't want him. They dismissed him. They told him he didn't fit the mold. They closed the door before he ever had the chance to knock.
When he told me his story, something inside me tightened.

I knew that pain. I had lived that pain.
And in that moment, I made a vow—a promise I felt deep in my bones.
I would not build my agency the way my old company built theirs.
I would not shut doors. I would not judge by résumé. I would not demand perfection. I would not turn away potential because it didn't look "corporate enough."
Instead, I decided:
If someone had a license, was willing to invest in themselves, and had a humble heart ready to learn— I would give them a shot.
That became my rule. My standard. My culture.
Because greatness isn't determined by credentials. It's determined by character.
So I hired him—my first producer.
And the moment I did, two emotions hit me at once:
Pride. And fear.
Pride because I was building something real. Fear because, for the first time, someone was counting on me.
Leadership is heavy—far heavier than any quota could ever be.
But leadership is also holy. A responsibility God places on those He intends to sharpen.
And I was being sharpened.

The Silent War Between Who I Was and Who I Was Becoming
Every day in March felt like a quiet battleground.
The old Steven—bruised, fearful, doubting—pulled backward. The new Steven—disciplined, steady, rising—pushed forward.
Some days I felt strong. Other days fear gripped my chest.
But every night, no matter how the day ended, I reminded myself:
A man who has already lost everything has nothing left to fear.
And that truth carried me through.

The Moment I Realized I Was Changing
One evening, after a long day of calls, training, studying, and planning, I sat alone at my desk.
Papers scattered. Notes everywhere. My notebook full. My producer's onboarding materials stacked neatly beside me.
And I paused.
I looked around and realized:
I am leading. I am building. I am responsible for others now.
It wasn't pride that filled my chest.
It was gratitude.
I wasn't healed completely. I wasn't confident every day. I wasn't successful yet.
But I was becoming something new.

The Weight and the Wonder
Late one night, as the house slept, I leaned back and closed my eyes.
The weight of leadership rested on my shoulders—heavy, unfamiliar, sacred.
But beneath that weight was wonder.
The wonder of a man who had lost everything and somehow found himself again.
In the glow of the desk lamp, with tomorrow waiting and my future unwritten, I whispered:
"Lord, if You open the doors, I will walk through them. Just don't let me waste the calling."
And I knew:
This wasn't rebuilding. This wasn't surviving.
This was the beginning of a legacy— one stone at a time.

Responsibility has a way of exposing a man.

It doesn't announce itself loudly. It settles in quietly, showing up in small decisions—how early you wake up, how thoroughly you prepare, how carefully you speak to someone who trusts you.

I felt that weight daily.

Not as pressure from above, but as accountability from within.

Every choice I made now echoed outward. Every mistake had consequences not just for me, but for someone learning under my guidance. That realization forced me to slow down, to think deeper, to lead with intention instead of impulse.

And slowly, without realizing it, my posture changed.

I spoke with more clarity. I listened more carefully. I stopped pretending I had all the answers.

Leadership wasn't about being right.

It was about being present.

There were moments I missed the simplicity of being told what to do.

Clear expectations. Defined lanes. Someone else responsible for the outcome.

But those moments passed.

Because simplicity comes at a cost.

And I had already paid it once.

This time, I was willing to carry complexity in exchange for ownership.

What I was building wasn't fast.

But it was solid.

Brick by brick. Decision by decision. Conversation by conversation.

And that kind of foundation doesn't crack easily.

I didn't know how big the structure would become. I only knew one thing for certain:

If the foundation was built right, it would hold.

And for the first time in my career, I wasn't rushing to prove anything.

I was taking the time to build something worth standing on.

That patience would change everything.
Because this time, I was building to last.
Not just for myself, but for everyone who would come after me.
That responsibility humbled me—and strengthened me.
Every solid structure begins unseen, below the surface.
What I was laying down in those weeks would support far more than I yet understood.
It was quiet work, but it was sacred work.
And I showed up for it every single day.
Because legacy is never built in moments of applause.
It is built in obedience, discipline, and faith when no one is watching.
That was the season I was in.
And I honored it.
It was the right beginning.
The only one that could have led me forward.
And I knew it.

Chapter 7: Momentum, Mercy, and the Making of a Brand

Spring arrived quietly—no parade, no lightning bolt, no obvious sign that my life was changing.
But something was shifting under the surface.
Something steady. Something sacred. Something earned.
For the first time since leaving the captive world, I didn't feel like a man running from the past.
I felt like a man building a future.
And the truth is this:
Momentum rarely announces itself. It grows one faithful act at a time.

The Second Agent — A Blessing I Never Expected
By May, something happened that still means more to me than most victories I've had since.
My mother—retired after decades as a purchaser for a large utility company—called me one morning and said:
"Steven… I've been watching you. Your ambition, your persistence, your fire. If you'll have me, I want to get my license and help lighten the load."

She said it casually.

But to me, it felt like validation straight from Heaven.

She didn't just want a job. She wanted to stand with me—shoulder to shoulder—in the agency I was fighting to build.

Her decision restored something inside me that I thought had been permanently broken:

The belief that I was worth following.

Leadership looks different when it comes from someone who knows you better than anyone else. Someone who has seen your failures, your doubts, your fears—and still chooses to stand beside you.

She will never fully understand what that meant to me.

But it remains one of the greatest honors of my early agency life.

Old-School Salesmanship in a World That Forgot People

By late spring, I realized something astonishing.

I wasn't winning because I was cheaper. I wasn't winning because I was faster. I wasn't winning because I had the biggest brand behind me.

I was winning because I treated people like human beings in an industry that had forgotten how.

While competitors hid behind scripts to justify rate increases, I listened.

While others tried to "manage objections," I acknowledged pain.

When clients vented about rising premiums, I understood—deeply.

What they didn't know was that I, too, was living on faith and the last few dollars in my bank account.

But I never asked for pity.

I listened. I slowed down. I let people speak.

And then I would say:

"We have two choices. But before we choose anything, tell me what you want your insurance to accomplish."

Clients would pause.

No one had ever asked them that before.

Then I guided them gently through the reality:

"Yes, rates increased. They may rise again someday. But if you'd like, we can shop around. Just know that every choice comes with trade-offs."

I'd smile and add:

"This is your picnic. I'm just setting out the meal."

And when the moment called for it, I shared the old truth my grandfather taught me:

"You can have cheap, fast, or good—but you only get to pick two."

There was nothing flashy about it.

Just honesty. Patience. Respect.

A listening ear still changes more hearts than a clever script ever will.

The First Office — A Gift From God Through a Neighbor

Around that same time, a local realtor—a client and respected businesswoman—reached out to me.

She was upgrading her independent brokerage to REMAX and discovered she needed Cyber Insurance.

None of the other agencies in town could help her.

I could.

After I secured her coverage, she looked at me and said:

"Steven, we'd make a great team."

Not long after, she offered me a small office space inside her brokerage—right next to the local coffee shop.

It wasn't just an office.

It was an introduction. A doorway. A lifeline.

She probably never realized what that offer meant.

Not just for my agency. But for my confidence. For my identity as a business owner.

For five years, I had served on the Economic Development
Committee, only to step down because scarcity thinking dominated the
room.
And here was a fellow entrepreneur who believed in abundance. Who
believed in partnership. Who opened a door that changed everything.
Ironically, she later filled the very seat I had resigned from.
But this time, that seat belonged to someone who believed in building
others up.

Becoming the Expert — Even Before I Felt Like One
My first group health case wasn't large.
But it mattered.
It was the first group plan issued within our entire firm.
Suddenly, I became "the group health guy."
Agents asked questions. Leadership noticed my name.
And even though we didn't have a dedicated farm and ranch market,
word spread that I knew that space too—because in my previous life,
it had been my signature.
People began seeking me out not because I had the most years in the
independent world, but because I carried myself like someone who
belonged.
And when I look back on that season, one truth rises above everything
else:
Leadership isn't assigned. Greatness isn't granted. Success doesn't ask
for permission.
They are claimed through action. Earned through integrity. Proven in
quiet moments— when no one is watching but God.
The Turning Point
One warm May evening, long after the phones stopped ringing and the
town settled into its nighttime hush, I sat alone in my tiny new office.
Lights low. Papers scattered. The smell of fresh coffee drifting through
the wall from the shop next door.

My mother's licensing books sat neatly stacked beside my own. My
first producer's notes lay open. My computer screen glowed softly
with tomorrow's plans.
And for the first time since the morning I carried a cardboard box out
of my old agency, I didn't feel broken.
I didn't feel forgotten. I didn't feel lost.
I felt called.
I leaned back in my chair and whispered:
"Lord… thank You for trusting me with this."
And in that quiet space, I understood something clearly.
This wasn't the rebuilding of a fallen man.
This was the rise of the man I was always meant to be.
And in that small office next to a coffee shop in a one-light Texas
town, my legacy—my real legacy—quietly began.

Momentum doesn't come from big wins. It comes from consistency.
Day after day, I showed up with the same intent—to serve well, to
listen closely, and to treat every conversation as if it mattered. Because
it did.
Mercy became part of my brand long before I ever named it.
I extended grace to clients frustrated by rate hikes. Patience to
prospects who needed time. Understanding to people who felt
overwhelmed.
In doing so, I realized something powerful:
People don't remember what you sell them. They remember how you
made them feel.

The Making of a Brand
I wasn't trying to "build a brand."
I was trying to build trust.
The brand emerged naturally—from consistency, humility, and service.

Word traveled quietly through town: "He listens." "He explains things clearly." "He doesn't rush you."

That reputation mattered more than any logo or tagline ever could.

It wasn't marketing. It was character.

And character compounds.

Grace Under Pressure

There were still hard days.

Days when deals fell through. Days when doubt returned. Days when exhaustion whispered that it would be easier to quit.

But momentum carried me forward.

Not because I was strong—but because I stayed faithful.

Every small victory stacked upon the last.

And slowly, unmistakably, the future I was building began to feel real.

Looking back, I can see that season clearly now.

Momentum taught me discipline. Mercy taught me humility. And the making of a brand taught me patience.

Nothing was rushed. Nothing was forced.

It was being shaped—slowly, deliberately—into something real.

And that was exactly how it needed to be.

Working alongside my mother added a layer of accountability I never expected.

I watched her study at the kitchen table with the same discipline she had carried through her entire career. No shortcuts. No excuses. Just steady effort. Seeing her invest her time and trust into something I had created forced me to raise my own standards.

I wasn't just building an agency anymore. I was stewarding trust.

That realization shaped how I answered phones, how I followed up, how I spoke about competitors, and how I treated people who could offer me nothing in return.

That was when I finally understood something about brand.
A brand isn't a slogan. It isn't a logo. It isn't a social media post.
A brand is the reputation you build when no one is watching. It is how you act when it costs you something. It is whether your word means something when walking away would be easier.
Without realizing it, I had begun to live by a principle that would later define everything I built:
Ride for your brand.
Not with noise. Not with ego. But with loyalty, humility, and relentless consistency.

Momentum carried me forward, but mercy kept me grounded.
Every win reminded me how close I had come to losing everything.
Every opportunity reminded me that none of this was guaranteed.
That awareness didn't weaken me. It anchored me.
And anchored men don't drift.

Chapter 8: Becoming the Leader I Never Expected

There comes a moment in every man's life when he realizes he is no longer who he was—and not yet who he will become.

A strange middle place. A holy tension. A season where the old self has fallen away, but the new self has not fully arrived.

That was me in early summer.

I wasn't a broken man crawling out of the ashes anymore. But I wasn't the fully risen man either.

I was something in between— a man being refined, reshaped, awakened.

Leadership was stirring in me long before I recognized it.

The Whisper of Leadership

It began quietly.

A phone call here. A text message there. A producer asking how I handled a difficult underwriting question. An agency owner wanting advice on quoting strategy. Another needing encouragement. Another needing clarity.

Then more calls. More messages. More voices turning toward me as if I carried answers I didn't yet know I possessed.

At first, I assumed it was coincidence.

By the tenth call, I felt humbled.

By the fortieth, something shifted inside me—not pride, not ego, but responsibility.

These men and women weren't reaching out because of my title. They were reaching out because of my scars. Because of the battles I had survived. Because when I spoke, I didn't speak from a script—I spoke from truth.

They weren't drawn to information. They were drawn to strength. Strength forged through loss. Through fire. Through a December I once feared would break me.

I didn't become a leader that summer.

I discovered I already was one.

The Weight of a Growing World

But leadership never comes alone.

It brings weight—real weight.

My phone became an extension of my hand. Emails multiplied faster than I could answer. Producer questions stacked atop client needs. Carrier reps wanted updates. Opportunities appeared. Fires needed extinguishing.

Some days the adrenaline fueled me. Some days I woke up ready to conquer the world. Some days I felt ten feet tall.

Other days I felt like a fraud.

The hardest moments weren't the busy ones. They were the quiet ones.

Late nights. The house asleep. The glow of the monitor. Hands pressed against my eyelids. A whisper into the silence:

"God… am I truly enough for all this?"

The truth was this:

I wasn't overwhelmed because I was drowning. I was overwhelmed because I was growing.

Growth aches. Growth stretches. Growth exposes. Growth heals by pulling a man beyond what he once believed possible.

I hadn't stepped into abundance. I had been pushed into it.

The Shift From Agent to Owner
Then came the day everything changed.
No lightning. No dramatic revelation. Just a moment—small, quiet, holy.
I sat at my desk surrounded by notes, quotes, carriers, renewal lists, producer onboarding plans, and a calendar so full it looked like a war map.
And suddenly the truth settled into me like a steady flame:
I am not an agent anymore. I am an owner.
Not just of a business.
Of my time. My decisions. My failures. My rise. My name. My destiny.
Agents wait to be told what to do. Owners build what needs to be built.
Agents react. Owners create.
Agents fear the unknown. Owners walk into it.
That day, I crossed an invisible line I could never uncross.

June — The Birth of the Writer
Then June arrived—and with it, a calling I never expected.
It came during a four-hour drive home from my second agency owners meeting. The sky streaked with gold. The road stretching endlessly forward. The tires humming beneath me like a steady heartbeat.
Earlier that day, another agency owner laughed and said:
"Steven, you're a fountain of knowledge. Why haven't you written a book?"
I laughed on the outside.
But inside, something cracked open.
His words echoed mile after mile: A book. Your story. Your lessons.
And then came the conviction—sharp and honest:

How can I preach abundance to my producers while hiding from my own?

I couldn't be a hollow leader. I couldn't say "take risks" while playing safe. I couldn't say "share your story" while hiding mine.

Leadership demands obedience. Obedience demands courage.

Somewhere between San Antonio and home, I decided:

I would write a book.

Not for attention. Not for applause. But to tell the truth. To bleed on paper so others wouldn't have to bleed alone.

Writing wasn't easy.

It forced me back into December. Back into wounds I'd sealed shut. Back into fears I buried.

Some nights I wrote one sentence. Some nights I wrote a page. Some nights I wrote nothing.

But I kept writing.

Because leaders aren't forged in comfort. They're forged in truth.

When the Past Began to Follow My Voice

Then something unexpected happened.

Not only did new agency owners reach out— former agents from my old captive company did too.

Competitors. Mentors. Peers. People I once believed stood above me. Now they asked for guidance.

"Steven, can we collaborate?" "How did you find momentum?"

"What's the independent model really like?" "Your story gives me hope."

We shared strategies. Referred clients. Solved problems together.

The people I once thought I wasn't good enough to stand beside were now walking with me.

True rising isn't about surpassing others. It's about becoming someone people trust to follow.

I was no longer just an agent.

I had become a leader— not because I claimed it, but because I lived it.

The Summer I Truly Rose
By August, the change was undeniable.
My agency was sprouting. My leadership was recognized.
My influence was expanding. My writing was becoming a mission.
I wasn't finished. I wasn't fully healed.
But I was standing taller than ever before.
One evening, after locking up my small office beside the coffee shop, I stepped into the thick Texas air.
Streetlights hummed. The scent of roasted beans lingered. The street stood quiet.
I caught my reflection in my truck window.
Not the man carrying a cardboard box. Not the man applying to hundreds of jobs. Not the man doubting his worth.
This man was different.
His shoulders were steady. His eyes were clear. His spirit aligned.
I whispered to the reflection:
"You're not going back."
The season of rebuilding had ended.
The season of becoming had begun.

Leadership has a way of revealing the cracks in a man long before it reveals his strengths.
Every conversation forced me to confront my own habits. Every question exposed gaps in my knowledge. Every request for guidance reminded me that people were watching how I responded—especially when I didn't know the answer.
That awareness didn't paralyze me. It disciplined me.
I began preparing more carefully. Speaking more intentionally. Listening more closely.

I learned that leadership isn't about always being right. It's about being responsible.

There were moments I missed anonymity.
Moments when it felt easier to blend into the background instead of standing out. Moments when I longed for fewer expectations and simpler days.
But those moments passed.
Because once a man steps into purpose, there is no returning to comfort.

Writing changed me as much as leadership did.
Putting words on paper forced honesty. It stripped away excuses. It demanded accountability.
I couldn't write about courage while avoiding it. I couldn't write about resilience without practicing it. I couldn't write about faith without living it.
The book became a mirror. And I couldn't look away.

What surprised me most was how leadership and writing fed each other.
The more I led, the more I understood. The more I wrote, the clearer my voice became.
Together, they reshaped me into someone stronger than I had ever been.

By the end of that summer, I understood something clearly.
Leadership isn't bestowed. It's revealed.
Not in moments of applause. But in seasons of obedience.
I didn't chase leadership. I responded to it.
And in doing so, I stepped fully into the man I was becoming.

The old fear that once ruled me had lost its grip.
Not because I was fearless. But because I had learned to move forward despite fear.
That distinction mattered.
Fear no longer dictated my decisions. Purpose did.
And once that shift happened, leadership stopped feeling accidental. It felt inevitable.

I didn't set out to become a leader.
I simply chose not to shrink anymore.
And that choice changed everything.
The man I was becoming could no longer hide behind hesitation.
He was called to stand.
And I finally did.

<u>**Part III – Small – Town Texas Values**</u>

Character is not made in a crisis — it is only exhibited.
Robert Freeman

Chapter 9: South Texas Roots — The Ground That Formed Me

There are places that raise a man… and there are places that forge him.

South Texas does both.

It is a land built on heat, hope, hardship, and honor. A land where thunderstorms roll in like entire armies, where droughts stretch out mercilessly, and where a man learns early that survival isn't a guarantee— it's an agreement between you, your faith, and the land beneath your boots.

Nothing about South Texas is gentle. But everything about it is honest.

Where Work Begins Before the Sun Does

Some boys grow up with summer vacations and lazy weekends. South Texas boys grow up knowing the land keeps its own calendar.

I didn't wake up early because I wanted to. I woke up early because the work needed doing. Help needed giving. Family needed hands on deck.

In winters when drought dug its claws deep into the soil and the mesquite thinned across the pastures, I watched my father run a torch across prickly pear cactus—burning away the needles so the cattle could eat without bleeding.

The flames glowed against the cold morning air. Orange sparks flickered like retreating fireflies. Ash drifted across the dirt. The cactus hissed and smoked as the needles curled into nothing.

It wasn't glamorous. It wasn't heroism.

It was necessary.

And necessary work is sacred work.

I didn't know it then, but burning cactus in the dead of winter was my first lesson in service.

Real service is doing what needs to be done—even when no one sees it, praises it, or thanks you for it.

The Classroom Without Walls

Some kids sit in neatly arranged desks learning from chalkboards and textbooks.

My classroom looked different.

It was the back of a flatbed trailer stacked with hay. A feed store with concrete floors that smelled like grain and sweat. A pasture alive with grasshoppers and heat waves. The shared labor of uncles and cousins pulling toward the same goal.

We didn't clock in. We didn't clock out. We showed up.

Because family needed us.

And in that unspoken obligation, a philosophy took root:

A person's value isn't in what they say. It's in what they do when the work is hard.

South Texas teaches a boy three lessons before manhood arrives:

Don't wait to be asked. If you see the need, step toward it.

Don't complain. Complaining wastes breath that work requires.

Don't measure yourself by applause. Service is its own reward—even when no one notices.

A Land That Teaches You How to Treat People

There's something about South Texas that softens a man's heart even while it hardens his hands.

When you grow up sweating alongside family—hurting together, laughing through exhaustion—you learn something simple and profound:

People are not transactions. They are relationships.

You treat a neighbor's fence like your own. You stop to help a stranger change a tire. You wave to passing trucks because, in small towns, there really aren't strangers.

Years later, when people sat across from me in my office venting about rate increases or whispering fears about protecting their families, I didn't reach for a script.

I reached for my upbringing.

I listened—really listened.

Because South Texas teaches you that a person's story matters more than their policy number.

You don't interrupt pain with talking points. You honor it. You sit with it.

Why No AI or Script Can Replace a South Texas Heart

Today, everyone talks about automation. Artificial intelligence. Chatbots. Algorithms.

You can automate tasks. You can automate data. You can automate reminders.

But you cannot automate truth. You cannot automate empathy. You cannot automate integrity.

No script understands the courage of a single mother watching her premium climb. No software feels the tremble in a widow's voice when she says, "I don't know how to do this without him."

People don't buy insurance from robots. They buy it from humans they trust.

South Texas raised me to be human first. Salesman second.

A Region That Builds Men Who Carry Their Name With Pride
In big cities, promotion comes from achievement. In South Texas, it comes from reputation.
Your name is your currency. Your word is your credit score. Your behavior writes your résumé every single day.
That truth followed me into adulthood more powerfully than any corporate training ever could.
It shaped how I answered phones. How I treated complaints. How I honored promises.
People trusted me not because I was perfect, but because I treated them the way my father treated the land—
With respect. With responsibility. With humility. With intention.

The Land That Lives Inside Me
In quiet moments now—after long days mentoring agents, writing, and building my agency—I close my eyes.
I still see the torch flame against winter air. I still smell the smoke of burnt cactus. I still feel hay scraping my arms. I still hear cattle lowing and cicadas singing.
That land is still shaping me.
Still grounding me. Still pushing me forward.
South Texas didn't just raise me.
It built the foundation of the man who would rise, rebuild, and ride for his brand.

Those early mornings and long days carved something permanent into me.
They taught me patience. They taught me humility. They taught me that effort, not entitlement, earns respect.

When you grow up tied to the land, you understand that results take time. Crops don't rush. Rain doesn't negotiate. And no amount of complaining changes the work required to bring something to life. That lesson followed me into adulthood.

It shaped how I approached my career. It shaped how I handled failure. It shaped how I treated success—never as something owed, but as something stewarded.

Faith was never separate from work in South Texas.

It wasn't something you spoke loudly about. It was something you lived.

You prayed for rain, then saddled up anyway. You asked for strength, then picked up the tools. You trusted God, but you still showed up. That balance—faith paired with responsibility—became the backbone of my life.

It taught me that belief without effort is hollow. And effort without belief is empty.

When I later entered the insurance world, I carried those values with me even when the environment didn't reward them.

I didn't chase shortcuts. I didn't oversell. I didn't promise what I couldn't deliver.

Because in South Texas, your name lives longer than any deal.

And I knew I would have to look people in the eye again—at the grocery store, at church, at the feed store, at the Friday night football game.

Reputation isn't an abstract idea there. It's daily accountability.

The land also taught me resilience.

Droughts didn't mean quitting. Storms didn't mean surrender. They meant adaptation.

You learned to bend without breaking. To endure without bitterness. To rebuild without resentment.

Those lessons carried me through seasons when my career faltered, when doors closed, and when uncertainty pressed in from every side. South Texas had already taught me how to stand when things got hard.

Even now, success hasn't erased those roots.
If anything, it's deepened them.
When the world gets loud, I still return to quiet. When pressure rises, I still remember necessity. When pride whispers, I still picture a torch burning cactus before sunrise.
That image keeps me grounded.
Because no matter how far I go, I know where I came from.

South Texas didn't just shape my childhood.
It shaped my conscience. It shaped my leadership. It shaped my understanding of service.
And everything I build today stands on that ground.
When people ask me where my approach to leadership comes from, they often expect a book title or a seminar name.
The truth is simpler.
It comes from watching men show up when no one was watching. From seeing families work without complaint. From learning that dignity is earned quietly.
South Texas didn't teach me how to sell.
It taught me how to stand.
And that has made all the difference.

Those roots still guide my steps.
They remind me that leadership without humility rots. That success without service hollows a man. And that growth without gratitude eventually collapses.
South Texas made sure I learned that early.

And I carry it with me—everywhere I go.
It is the ground I stand on.
The soil that shaped my spine.
The place that taught me who I am.
And why I will never forget it.
Because no matter how far a man travels, the land that raised him always calls him back—to remember, to remain humble, and to lead with heart.

Chapter 10 Community Is Currency

There is a special kind of wealth forged in small towns— a kind the world often overlooks because it can't be measured in bank accounts, prestige, or titles. It's measured in people. In trust. In the quiet bonds between families whose roots run deeper than any water well. In the way a community raises its children, protects its own, and teaches lessons no schoolbook ever could.

I was raised in not one, but two such communities: Kosciusko and Poth— two small South Texas towns whose values shaped every corner of my character. Each gave me something different. Each gave me something priceless.

And together, they forged in me a truth I would not fully appreciate until decades later:

In small towns, community is currency.

And if you honor that currency, it will carry you farther than any degree, talent, or résumé ever will.

Two Towns, One Upbringing

Kosciusko was where my story began— a Polish farming community stitched together by family names, Sunday Mass, and fields that stretched toward every horizon.

Poth was where my story grew— a school of barely forty students per grade, taught by teachers who weren't just educators, but alumni who returned home to pour into the next generation.

In big cities, teachers may come and go. In Poth, teachers stayed. They didn't just teach us. They loved us. Corrected us. Guided us. Protected us.

They were living proof that the phrase "It takes a village to raise a child"

is not a cliché. It is a way of life.

In our small towns, your mom often knew what you did before you got home. Not because someone wanted to catch you— but because everyone wanted to protect you.

Your neighbors. Your friends' parents. Your coaches. Your teachers. They all played a role in shaping you— keeping you straight, humble, respectful, and accountable.

There is no anonymity in places like ours. And thank God for that. Because anonymity doesn't build character. Community does.

The Land That Remembers

My family's farm in Kosciusko— land held by my mother's family since they first came to America— was more than acreage.

It was inheritance. It was identity. It was the living memory of generations who worked before sunrise and rested long after sunset.

As a boy, I learned work the way most kids learn games— by watching, copying, and eventually keeping pace with the men around me.

I helped my father haul hay to cattle in the biting winter cold. I watched uncles slice and burn prickly pear cactus so the cattle could eat during droughts that stretched into winter months. I worked alongside cousins fixing fences, clearing brush, and learning to endure the elements without complaint.

No one gave speeches. No one asked if you felt like helping.

You simply stepped in— because that's what family does.

Those fields— with their rows of crops, their open pastures, their ancient mesquite trees— taught me lessons no classroom ever could: That service is sacred. That a good name matters more than money. That every generation owes something to the next. That hard work is not punishment— it is privilege.

Even now, as an adult, I return to that land every week. Not out of obligation, but out of reverence.

A Steward of Two Homes

I live in Poth now, the place that raised me just as surely as the farm did.

Here, I've served as a City Councilman for more than a decade— a responsibility that has shaped me as deeply as the land itself.

Leadership in a small town isn't political. It's personal.

Here, you don't serve ideas. You serve people.

You don't protect borders. You protect families.

You don't speak for "constituents." You speak for neighbors. Friends. Childhood classmates. Elders who once watched over you.

Every vote carries a face. Every decision carries a name.

When I cast a vote, I do it with one question above all else:

"Will this protect the world my children will inherit?"

Because I am not only raising three children— I am standing guard over the values that will raise them.

Values passed down through my mother's family and the land they stewarded. Values passed down through the halls of Poth ISD and the teachers who shaped me. Values passed down through elders in Kosciusko who believed community mattered more than individual gain.

Now, I am a steward of those same values— for my children, for my neighbors, for my town.

I stand in the same fields my ancestors once walked. I stand in the same council chambers where Poth's future is shaped.

Two homes. Two inheritances. One purpose:

To preserve the world that preserved me.

The Weight of What We Carry

Some evenings, after the sun sinks behind the South Texas horizon and the world grows quiet, I stand on my mother's family land— the same earth that fed cattle, grew crops, and raised children long before I was born.

The grass shifts in the breeze. The dirt holds the footprints of generations.

And in the fading gold of dusk, I feel the weight of something humbling and holy:

I am the bridge between the past and the future. I am the keeper of values that shaped me. The guardian of a community that raised me. The steward of land my children will inherit. The protector of a small-town way of life that built the man I have become.

In that quiet, I whisper a truth I've come to cherish:

Community is not where you live. Community is who you become because of it.

And I pray that when my children are grown and walk this land with their own families, they feel what I feel now— the profound blessing of belonging to a place that never stopped believing in them.

Small towns remember.

They remember who showed up. They remember who helped when no one was watching. They remember who cut corners—and who refused to.

That memory becomes accountability.

In a place like Poth or Kosciusko, you can't hide behind a logo or a title. You carry your reputation everywhere you go— into church pews, grocery aisles, ball fields, and city meetings.

That kind of visibility does something powerful to a person. It forces honesty. It demands consistency. It rewards integrity over time.

Community also teaches restraint.

In small towns, success isn't something you flaunt. It's something you steward.

You learn early that rising too fast or boasting too loudly fractures trust. So you move carefully. Gratefully.

Aware that every blessing carries responsibility.

That mindset shaped how I built my agency. How I hired. How I served. How I led.

I wasn't trying to be the biggest name. I was trying to be a good one. Community is also forgiveness.

In small towns, people know your mistakes. They remember your missteps.

But if you own them, learn from them, and keep showing up, they give you room to grow.

That grace taught me how to lead others— not with perfection, but with patience.

As my career evolved, those lessons became more valuable than any marketing strategy.

Trust compounds. Reputation appreciates. Relationships outlast transactions.

That is the quiet economy of small towns.

When people ask me how I built influence without a massive platform or budget, this is my answer:

I invested in people. I honored the community. And I treated trust like currency— spending it wisely, earning it slowly, and never taking it for granted.

In a world chasing scale and speed, small towns still teach the power of depth.

Depth of relationship. Depth of commitment. Depth of character.

And that depth has carried me further than anything else ever could.

If the world ever forgets what real wealth looks like, small towns will remember.

Because wealth isn't built only in boardrooms. It's built in backyards.
On front porches. In council chambers. At church suppers. And on
land passed from one generation to the next.
Community is currency. And I will spend my life honoring it.

Chapter 11 Land, Quiet Mornings, and the Smell of Fresh-Cut Fields

There are places in this world that shape a man quietly—not with speeches or instructions, but with the language of the land whispered into him long before he understands what he's learning.
For me, that place will forever be South Texas.
Long before I ever walked into an office, long before insurance became a career, long before I knew what hurt or rebuilding meant, the land was teaching me what strength, humility, and belonging felt like.
Even now, if I close my eyes, I can smell it: the sweetness of fresh-cut hay, the deep, earthy scent of freshly plowed fields, and the familiar perfume of South Texas clay warming under the morning sun.
Those smells don't just remind me of where I come from. They remind me of who I am.
Quiet mornings taught me patience. They taught me how to listen. They taught me how to lead without noise.
City people think quiet means nothing is happening. But in the country, quiet is full. Quiet is alive.

Quiet is the hum of cicadas rising with the heat. Quiet is cattle sounding off across distant pastures. Quiet is birds gliding from pecan limb to pecan limb. Quiet is frogs chirping from hidden pockets of brush. Quiet is thick, humid air settling over black land soil, carrying the scent of clay baked all day under the fierce Texas sun.

Quiet is where a boy becomes a man, because there are no distractions to hide behind.

In that stillness, you hear your thoughts—your doubts, your hopes, your convictions—long before anyone else does.

Two scents shaped my childhood more than any others: fresh-cut fields and fresh-plowed earth.

Fresh-cut fields smell like preparation, responsibility, and cattle moving across green acres. Fresh-plowed soil smells deeper—like hope, like possibility, like the world turning itself over to make room for something better.

Growing up around that teaches you a truth most people miss: growth always begins underground long before anyone sees the results.

I carried that lesson into adulthood, into business, into leadership, and into rebuilding. If you quit because nothing looks different yet, you never gave growth enough time.

No smell in this world carries me home faster than the Cibolo Creek bottom on a hot South Texas summer day.

The air there is heavy. The soil is dark. The water moves slow but steady.

The creek teaches patience. It teaches persistence. It teaches adaptation.

It flows whether you are strong or broken, confident or afraid, winning or rebuilding. And somehow, that steadiness heals.

Growing up near the Cibolo gave me a respect for water—not because of its force, but because of its nature.

Water adapts. It bends. It finds new routes when old paths close.

It doesn't demand the way. It earns it.

It doesn't overpower obstacles. It outlasts them.

Over time, I realized water is the greatest teacher I've known—and the greatest salesman too.

A man who refuses to adapt will drown in stubbornness. A man who keeps flowing quietly, steadily, faithfully will carve his place into the world.

Water that stops moving becomes stagnant. So does a man.

The older I get, the more I realize the land wasn't just shaping me for work or leadership. It was shaping me for fatherhood.

Land teaches patience. Seeds do not grow on demand. Neither do children.

You don't force growth. You protect it. You nourish it. You show up every day, especially when progress feels invisible.

When I walk those fields now, I don't just see my past. I see my children's future.

I imagine them learning the same lessons I did—not through lectures, but through presence. Through early mornings. Through quiet observation. Through watching how a man treats the ground beneath his feet.

The land taught me that my job as a father isn't to control my children. It's to steward them.

To prepare the soil of their hearts. To pull the weeds before they choke what's good. To teach them that effort matters more than entitlement, and that character grows best when no one is watching.

In South Texas, the land doesn't coddle. It doesn't apologize for heat or drought. But it always gives back when treated with respect.

That's the kind of father I strive to be—firm but fair, steady not loud, present not perfect.

I don't want my children to remember speeches. I want them to remember consistency.

I want to be the kind of man they can return to when life gets heavy—
steady, rooted, unmoving in my values.

Some people inherit money. Some inherit property.

I inherited land that remembers.

Land that remembers my mother's family. The generations who trusted this soil with their future. The hands that worked it. The faith that sustained it.

When life knocked me flat and I returned unsure of myself, the land knew.

It didn't rush me. It didn't question me. It waited.

The land raised me once as a boy, and it raised me again as a man.

One evening, as the sun melted into the horizon and the clay still radiated the heat of the day, I walked down to the creek alone.

Cicadas hummed. Frogs echoed. Cattle called from far pastures. And the Cibolo whispered its slow, steady truth.

I stood there—hurt, healing, rebuilding—and the air smelled of clay and water, of childhood and manhood, of where I had been and where I was going.

And in that quiet, the land spoke what my spirit had been aching to hear:

You are not lost. You are being rebuilt.

I breathed it in and knew with certainty: I was returning to my roots not to stay where I had been, but to become who I was meant to be.

Because land—real land—doesn't just grow crops.

It grows character. It grows courage. It grows resilience. It grows men who rise again.

And as long as the Cibolo keeps flowing, I know I will too.

Chapter 12 Learning to Work With Your Hands First

Before I ever learned how to persuade, before I ever learned how to
sell, mentor, or lead, I learned how to work.
Not the sanitized kind of work that fits neatly on a résumé. Not
busywork designed to make a man feel productive. Not tasks
measured by keystrokes, meetings, or metrics.
I learned the kind of work that stains your shirt, soaks your hat with
sweat, burns your shoulders, and forces you to confront who you
really are when no one is watching.
Work shaped me long before ambition ever claimed me. Long before
confidence. Long before titles. Long before leadership.
Work came first.
A Father's Hands, A Father's Gospel
My father grew up as one of eight children in a farming family that
survived not on abundance, but on grit. Nothing was wasted. Nothing
was handed out freely. Everything had to be earned.
He was a man built from necessity—quiet, steady, and unmoved by
long days or hard seasons. He didn't romanticize labor, but he
respected it. He understood work the way some men understand

prayer: something practiced daily, without fanfare, because it sustains life.

He rose before dawn, worked a full shift, and still ended each evening sitting high on a tractor seat, framed against a South Texas sunset, with only the hum of the engine and the wide-open sky to keep him company.

I watched him from the ground as a boy, dust clinging to my jeans, sun pressing against my neck, learning without realizing that leadership begins long before anyone ever notices you.

He never complained. He never begged for easier days. He never once acted as though the work owed him anything.

He lived by a truth many men spend their entire lives avoiding: Nothing worth having comes without sweat. And no good man asks for a lighter load—only a stronger back.

I learned my work ethic by watching him. By matching my footsteps to his across fields and pastures. By carrying more than I thought I could, because quitting was never modeled as an option. By seeing what it looked like when a man gave everything he had to his family without expecting applause.

His hands were cracked and strong, worn smooth by years of labor. They carried the weight of responsibility without drama. They taught me how a man shows love without ever speaking the word.

Return With Me to the Summers That Built Me

If you want to understand what real work ethic is, return with me to the summers of South Texas. Summers that didn't ask if you were ready. Summers that arrived heavy with heat and expectation.

Return with me to the fields where we hauled square bales. Not round bales lifted effortlessly by tractors. Square bales. Heavy. Awkward. Unforgiving.

One man on the trailer. One man on the ground. One rhythm: lift, throw, stack, sweat. Repeat.

You didn't stop because you were hot—everyone was hot. You didn't stop because sweat burned your eyes or ants bit your legs. You didn't stop because your arms shook or your back screamed.

You stopped when the field was done.

Many nights that meant working by moonlight, fireflies blinking across the pasture, coyotes calling from the distant tree line. Exhaustion was not an excuse. It was simply part of the cost.

Those fields taught me patience. They taught me accountability. They taught me that effort compounds quietly, long before results ever show themselves.

Work Teaches Humility

The sun does not negotiate. The land does not shorten its demands because your muscles ache. Nature does not bend to comfort.

Work humbles a man long before life ever does.

It shows you there are no small tasks—only tasks you are too proud to appreciate. It strips ego quickly and replaces it with respect for effort. The land corrected my pride. The labor corrected my impatience. The summers corrected my sense of entitlement.

Humility grew quietly in places where no applause was expected and no reward was guaranteed. That kind of humility stays with you. It shapes how you speak, how you listen, and how you lead others.

Work Teaches Respect

Working alongside my father, uncles, and cousins taught me that respect is not demanded—it is earned through shared burden.

When you sweat beside someone, titles disappear. Status fades. What remains is character.

That lesson followed me into business. Clients trusted me because they could feel it. Producers listened because they recognized it. Relationships formed because people knew I wasn't afraid of effort. People can sense whether you were raised on responsibility or raised on excuses.

Work Teaches Endurance

Farm work teaches endurance without theatrics. No speeches. No drama. No quitting.

Weather ruins plans. Equipment breaks. Cattle still need feeding. Fields still need cutting.

You adapt or you fail.

Years later, when my career collapsed and fear crept in, it wasn't motivation that carried me forward. It was muscle memory.

You've worked tired before. You've worked hurting before. You've worked scared before.

Get up. Keep going. The field isn't done yet.

Work Teaches Gratitude

You cannot work the land without learning gratitude.

A cool breeze feels like mercy. Water tastes like blessing. A tractor shutting off at dusk feels like grace. A tailgate becomes a throne for tired bones.

Gratitude becomes perspective. Perspective becomes humility. Humility becomes strength.

The Work Prepared Me

When I lost everything years later, people asked how I endured.

They assumed resilience. But it wasn't learned in that moment. It was remembered.

The boy who hauled hay became the man who rebuilt from nothing. The field had already trained me.

The Hands That Worked Became the Hands That Lead

One night, after a long day running my agency, I paused and looked down at my hands.

Hands shaped by labor. Hands shaped by discipline. Hands shaped by example. Hands that once stacked hay now building something meant to last beyond me.

And the truth settled in:

Leadership did not make me a worker. Work made me a leader.

The greatest leaders are not forged in boardrooms. They are forged in fields. In sweat. In sacrifice. In silence.
I thank God that before He ever asked me to lead, He taught me to work.
Because a man who learns to work will always know how to rise.

Chapter 13 Winning People, Not Just Sales

Before I ever carried a business card, before I ever learned
underwriting, before I ever sat across from a client explaining
coverage, I learned the greatest truth a salesman can ever know:
A person's heart cannot be won by force—only by honor.
Numbers may keep a business alive, but people give that business a
soul. Without trust, sales are temporary. Without integrity, success is
borrowed time.
Somewhere between the fields of Kosciusko and the hallways of Poth
High School, I learned that service is not a technique or a tactic. It is
an inheritance—passed down like a family story, carried quietly in the
character of the people who raised me.
Where I Learned the Way
Before insurance, before leadership, before City Centre, there was
simply a boy watching the world around him.
I watched men who shook hands with conviction and meant every
word they said. Men who understood a handshake was not a
formality—it was a promise. Women who cooked for neighbors
before cooking for themselves. Families who showed up whether it
was convenient or not.

In our corner of South Texas, integrity wasn't taught in a classroom. You breathed it in the air. You saw it in the fields. You felt it in the pews of St. Ann's. You lived it in the quiet ways people showed up for one another without expecting recognition.

When you looked someone in the eye, you acknowledged their dignity. And dignity demanded respect.

It was never lectured. It was lived. And that truth became the backbone of every sale I would ever make.

The Unteachable Advantage

During my captive years, I watched agents cling to scripts like life rafts in a storm. I understood why. Scripts feel safe. Predictable. Controlled. But scripts cannot see fear in a mother's eyes when she talks about protecting her children. Scripts cannot hear the tremble in a retiree's voice when he says the premium went up again. Scripts cannot feel the exhaustion in a single parent trying to stretch every dollar.

People don't want perfection. They want presence.

They want to feel understood—not managed, not maneuvered, not handled.

So while others rehearsed lines, I chose to listen. Sometimes through anger. Sometimes through tears. Sometimes through silence that stretched uncomfortably long—long enough for a person to stop performing and start telling the truth.

And in those moments, I learned something no training manual ever taught me:

Listening is the most powerful sales tool ever created—and it costs nothing.

A Tale of Two Agents

I remember a day early in my career when a customer called in hot. Premium up. Payday week already tight. Children at home. A car that "needed something" and a refrigerator that "was making that sound again."

I could hear it in her breathing. She wasn't mad at me. She was mad at life.

I happened to be sitting near another agent who had his script printed and highlighted. He meant well. He was trying to do his job the way he was trained. He leaned over and whispered, "Just empathize and pivot to the bundle. That's what they want."

He wasn't wrong—according to the playbook.

He took the call first.

I listened as he read the words like a checklist.

"I completely understand your frustration." "I'd feel the same way." "Unfortunately, these increases are industry-wide." "Let's explore your options."

Every line was technically correct. But it landed like cardboard.

The customer kept interrupting. Her voice rose. She felt like she was being managed instead of heard.

When she hung up, she didn't say "thank you." She said, "I'll call back." The kind of call-back that never comes.

I called her later that afternoon—not with a script, but with curiosity.

"Ma'am," I said, "before we talk numbers, tell me what this increase does to your month. What does it actually change for you?"

She went quiet. Then she exhaled like a person who had been holding her breath all day.

She told me about her kid's dentist appointment. The groceries. The overtime that got cut. The fear of being one more bill away from a spiral.

I didn't rush her.

When she finished, I said, "Thank you for telling me the truth. Now let's look at coverage and we'll make the best decision for your life—not the best decision for my quota."

That sentence wasn't clever. It was honest.

And honesty is what calms a nervous system.

That day I learned: people don't reject insurance. They reject feeling small.

Why I Refused to Sell What Wasn't Right

I was questioned more times than I can count.

Why didn't you push that policy? Why didn't you bundle the sale? You would have hit quota. You could have won the trip.

My answer never changed.

Because it wasn't right for the client.

To some, that made me naïve. To others, foolish.

But I knew something they didn't.

A dishonest sale haunts a man. An honest one lets him sleep at night.

Hard roads build strong men. Easy shortcuts build regret.

The Sale I Walked Away From

There were times integrity cost me. One in particular still stands out.

A family sat across from me with enough income and assets that I could have sold them a larger policy than they truly needed. The numbers worked. The approval was guaranteed. The commission would have helped me hit my goals.

Another agent would have closed it without hesitation.

But as they spoke, I could see the pressure they were already under—tuition, medical bills, an aging parent whose health was turning unpredictable. Under the words, there was a quiet fear about the future.

I could have sold more.

Instead, I told them the truth.

"This coverage will protect you," I said. "Anything beyond this would be nice—but it wouldn't be responsible. I want you protected, not stretched."

They thanked me and left.

No sale. No commission. No scoreboard recognition.

I sat at my desk after they walked out and felt that strange mix every honest salesman knows: disappointment in the bank account, peace in the chest.

That night, I went home lighter than I had arrived. Because I knew something important: I can lose money and still keep my character. But if I lose my character, no amount of money will ever be enough.

The Sale I Refused to Win

There was another moment that shaped me just as much.

A client called asking for "the cheapest possible." He didn't want to talk about risk. He didn't want to talk about liability. He wanted a number he could brag about.

In the captive world, that kind of sale was treated like a win.

But I had seen what "cheap" really means when the wind hits the wrong direction and something catches fire. I had seen what happens when a family realizes too late that the policy they bought wasn't protection—it was a receipt.

So I told him the truth, plainly.

"I can get you cheap," I said. "But if it doesn't protect you, it's not insurance. It's a false sense of security."

He got quiet, then defensive.

"I've been doing it this way for years," he said.

"I understand," I replied. "And I'm not here to insult you. But I'd rather lose this sale than sell you something I wouldn't sell my own family."

He didn't buy that day.

Two weeks later he called back, calmer.

"Alright," he said. "Show me the right way."

Sometimes the sale isn't won in the moment. Sometimes it's won when a person realizes you refused to take advantage of them.

The Day the Customer Brought a Gift

One ordinary Tuesday, a woman called angry about her rate. Her voice shook not from frustration, but fatigue—the kind that comes from life piling on all at once.

I let her vent. I didn't interrupt. I didn't defend. I didn't pretend I had magic words to fix her budget. I just listened like her story mattered—because it did.

When she ran out of steam, I said, "You're allowed to be tired. Let's figure this out together."

We reviewed coverage slowly. I explained trade-offs. I made sure she understood what she would lose if she cut too far. We shopped where we could. We kept what mattered.

The next day she returned—with lunch in one hand and a baby gift in the other.

"You listened," she said. "No one ever does."

She wasn't thanking an agent. She was thanking a human being.

People remember kindness longer than any rate you ever quote.

"This Is Your Picnic"—The Philosophy of Empowerment

I often told clients, "This is your picnic. I'm just setting the meal out." It put them where they belonged: in control.

Insurance isn't about coercion. It's about clarity. It's about laying out truth plainly so people feel empowered, not pressured. I would explain trade-offs like a neighbor, not a negotiator.

Then I'd add the old saying: "You can have cheap, fast, or good—but you only get two."

People appreciated honesty more than polish.

Honesty is a form of love. And people can tell when they are being loved.

Why Clients Followed Me

Looking back, people followed me because I did what I said I would do. I spoke to them like neighbors, not numbers. I called them back. I remembered their stories. I treated their questions like they mattered—because they did.

Clients don't stay for price. They stay for peace.

And peace is something you offer with your heart, not your commission structure.

The Wiatrek Way—Before I Knew Its Name

Long before I wrote a book, long before I spoke to audiences, long before I dared to call myself a leader, I lived this truth:

Win the person, and the sale will take care of itself.

No script can replace sincerity. No AI can replicate compassion. No algorithm can mimic integrity. No handbook can teach honor.

Those things must be lived—earned—practiced—carried in the quiet chamber of a man's soul.

Where Salesmanship and Spirit Become One

Some evenings, when the world presses in, I step onto my back porch and sit near the koi pond. The water glows in the last light of day. The fish move slowly, steadily—unhurried, unbothered—growing quietly with every passing season.

Their calm reminds me of the Cibolo: always flowing, always adapting, always moving forward—never rushing, never retreating.

And in that stillness, God whispers the same truth He has whispered to me since the beginning:

Growth takes time. Strength takes seasons. And every moment of kindness you give returns to you in ways you cannot predict.

So I rise from that bench strengthened—ready to serve again, to listen again, to honor again, to win people again.

Because in the end, sales fade. Policies lapse. Companies change.

But the way you treat people follows you forever.

<u>**Part IV – Family, Faith & Legacy**</u>

We are not the makers of history. We are made by history.
                    -    *Martin Luther King Jr.*

Chapter 14 The Weight of a Family Name

There are moments in a man's life when he becomes aware—truly aware—that he is not walking this world alone.
He carries more than his own hopes, his own fears, his own dreams.
He carries the quiet footsteps of those who came before him. He carries the echoes of voices he never heard, the calloused hands he never touched, the sacrifices he never witnessed—yet all of them live within him.
Some men spend their lives trying to build a name.
I was born into one.
Not a name of fortune. Not a name of prestige. But a name built on the humble, sacred soil of South Texas—by people who knew hardship as a daily companion and still rose every morning with grit stitched into their bones.
Both my mother's family and my father's family came from the same kind of backroads—roads where streetlights were replaced by stars, where neighbors weren't acquaintances but extended kin, and where your bloodline meant less than your character.
These were people who didn't talk about honor. They lived it.
They didn't speak of perseverance. They embodied it.

They didn't dream of ease. They prayed for strength.

And that strength carried them through storms that would have broken lesser men.

A Legacy Forged in Hard Seasons

Long before I ever stood on the land I now own, that land had already been shaped by the hands of my ancestors—hands weathered by sun and wind, hands familiar with reins, tools, and plows, hands that spoke through callouses instead of complaints.

During the Great Depression—a time when money evaporated, crops failed, and the future seemed to shrink smaller with every passing day—my ancestors refused to surrender.

When there wasn't enough food, they rationed. When the rains didn't come, they prayed. When the land dried and cracked beneath the punishing sun, they worked anyway.

They understood a truth few modern minds can fully grasp:

That which is worth keeping is worth suffering for.

Their survival was not guaranteed—it was earned. Not by one generation, but by many. Line upon line. Year upon year. Season upon season.

They planted trees they would never live long enough to see fully grown. They built barns their grandchildren would inherit. They tended soil that would feed families not yet born.

That—more than anything else—is legacy: Work done in faith for someone who does not yet exist.

But legacy is not romantic in the moment. It is exhausting. It is uncertain. It asks everything and promises nothing in return.

Yet they gave anyway.

Warriors Without Headlines

My mother's family sent sons off to war—World War I, World War II—not because they sought glory, but because duty called and character answered.

They returned quietly. Without parades. Without headlines.

They returned to fields that needed plowing, to cattle that needed tending, to families that needed love.

They carried war in their bones and grief in their prayers, yet still showed up the next morning to do what needed doing.

Heroes do not always wear medals. Some wear mud. Some wear sweat. Some wear the quiet dignity of men who understand that courage is not proven in moments of applause—but in decades of faithfulness.

My Place in the Lineage

Today, I walk those same fields—not as a visitor, not as an observer, but as a steward.

I have the privilege of owning a portion of the land that fed generations before me. When I stand on that soil, I do not feel like its master. I feel like its apprentice.

The land does not belong to me in the way modern culture defines ownership. It has been entrusted to me—for a time.

The wind that moves across those pastures carries more than the scent of South Texas grass. It carries whispers of men who stayed the course, women who held families together during impossible times, and children who grew into adults who built towns not with speeches, but with service.

Their lives are the foundation upon which mine now stands.

And that is why the weight of a family name is not a burden—it is a calling.

A name isn't something you inherit. A name is something you rise to meet.

Two Communities, One Legacy

Growing up between Kosciusko and Poth, I learned that community was not built by money or influence. It was built by ordinary people doing extraordinary things quietly.

Teachers in Poth—many of them alumni themselves—taught us not only academics, but values. They taught discipline, respect, humility, and how to carry ourselves with pride that didn't need to boast.

They corrected us when we were wrong. They celebrated us when we tried. They held us accountable because they believed we could be better.

In Kosciusko, my family's roots ran deep into the clay soil—roots that taught me that the measure of a man is not what he accumulates, but what he contributes.

Together, those two places shaped me into a man who understands that character is not optional—it is essential.

Legacy Is a Living Thing

Now, as a father, I see the world differently.

I no longer think only in days or years. I think in generations.

Every choice I make, every act of service, every sacrifice, every lesson I teach my children ripples forward into time—long after I am gone.

And as a City Councilman for more than a decade, I stand guard—not merely over budgets or policies—but over a way of life worth preserving.

Leadership in a small town is personal. You do not govern strangers. You serve neighbors. You protect families whose children play beside your own.

The small towns that raised me deserve leaders who understand that legacy is not born in meetings—it is born in hearts. It is sustained by families. It is carried by names.

The Weight Becomes Purpose

Some evenings, when the light softens and the world finally exhales, I step into my backyard and watch my children play.

Their laughter rises into the warm South Texas air like a hymn— untouched by worry, untouched by the burdens that wait for all of us in time.

And as I stand there quietly, I wonder if one day they will understand the weight of the name they carry—not as a chain, but as a compass.

Will they know of the men and women who came before them? Will they understand the droughts, the wars, the labor, the prayers? Will they feel, deep in their bones, that their bloodline was built on quiet courage—the kind that rises again and again until the work is done?

A child does not inherit character. He witnesses it. He absorbs it. He grows into it.

And I, their father, am writing the chapter they will one day read—not with words alone, but with choices, discipline, humility, and love.

So I stand there longer, breathing in the evening, and whisper a prayer: "Let me live in such a way that my children will understand why this name is worth carrying."

Because I cannot choose the world my children will inherit—but I can choose the man they see leading them into it.

Chapter 15 Becoming A Father Worth Emulating

There comes a moment in every father's life when the noise of the world quiets just long enough for a single truth to land with weight: Your children are watching you.

Not when life is polished. Not when you're posting wins. Not when you're at your best.

They are watching when you're tired. When you walk in the door carrying the day on your shoulders. When you're trying to smile through stress. When the pressure follows you home like a shadow. Especially then.

I didn't fully understand that at first. In those early months of rebuilding—when the agency was still young, the income wasn't steady yet, and the responsibility felt like a backpack full of rocks I was learning how to lead and provide at the same time. Some days I felt strong. Other days I felt stretched so thin I couldn't tell where "business owner" ended and "father" began.

Fatherhood doesn't wait until a man feels ready. It unfolds in real time, under real pressure, with real consequences.

Fatherhood Under Pressure

There were evenings I walked through the door carrying more than a briefcase. I carried unanswered emails, carrier issues, client problems that couldn't wait, and the kind of financial uncertainty that makes even a grown man stare at the ceiling at night.

I tried to leave it at the door. I rarely succeeded.

My children didn't know the details. They didn't know the numbers or the deadlines or the risks. But children don't need a spreadsheet to sense weight. They can feel it in a father's voice. They can read it in his posture. They can tell when his mind is still somewhere else, even when his body is sitting at the table.

That realization humbled me.

Because leadership at work might earn respect, but leadership at home earns legacy.

The Nights That Tested Me

Some of the hardest moments came late at night. The house quiet. The world finally still. The adrenaline gone. That's when the questions showed up—the ones you don't always admit out loud.

Am I doing enough? Am I present enough? Am I building something worth the time it's costing? Will they remember my effort… or my absence?

There were nights I sat on the edge of the bed and listened to the slow breathing of a sleeping child. I'd watch their chest rise and fall, and the weight of fatherhood would press deeper than any work problem ever could. In that stillness, the truth became undeniable:

My children don't need a perfect provider. They need a present father. And presence is costly. It costs your pride. It costs your schedule. It costs your urge to keep grinding when the people you love are asking, in their own way, "Are you here with us?"

The Battle Between Provision and Presence

Every father knows this tension. You want to give them everything—security, opportunity, stability, a future. You want to be the man who breaks cycles and builds something bigger than himself.

But the danger is this: you can become so focused on building a future that you forget to live in the present.

I've felt that temptation. The phone buzzes. The email comes in. The deal is close. The problem needs solving. And then you hear a little voice ask a simple question—"Dad, can you play?"—and you feel the pull in your chest.

The world praises the man who is always "on." A child remembers the man who was actually there.

There were moments I failed that test. I answered one more message. I chased one more task. I told myself, "In a minute," and that minute became the moment that passed. I'm not proud of it. But I'm grateful those failures taught me something: you don't fix fatherhood with intentions. You fix it with choices.

The Imperfect Father With Endless Love

I don't want my children to put me on a pedestal so high that I have to pretend to stay balanced up there. I want them to know I am human. I want them to see effort, not image.

I want them to see me apologize.

Because an apology from a father is a powerful thing. It teaches a child that strength is not the absence of mistakes—it is ownership of them. It teaches that humility is not weakness—it is integrity. It teaches that love does not disappear when you are wrong; it grows when you make it right.

There were nights I lost patience. Times I spoke sharper than I should have. Moments where the day's pressure spilled into the home like a storm cloud. And in those moments, I had a choice: defend myself or correct myself.

So I learned to kneel down. To look into small eyes. To say the words every man must learn if he wants to be worth emulating:

"I was wrong." "I'm sorry." "I'm going to do better."

And then I had to prove it—not with a grand gesture, but with a new pattern.

Life Lesson #1: Pressure Does Not Excuse Poor Character

I want my children to learn without me ever lecturing them that pressure does not give you permission to be harsh. Exhaustion does not justify bitterness. Responsibility is never an excuse to stop being kind.

I want them to see a man who works hard but does not worship work. A man who carries responsibility but does not carry resentment. A man who chases purpose but does not sacrifice peace on the altar of ambition.

Because if I teach them anything, I want it to be this: Character is what remains when life gets heavy.

Life Lesson #2: A Made-Up Mind Can Be Gentle

I grew up believing that determination meant toughness—keep going, don't complain, handle it. But fatherhood taught me a deeper form of strength: a made-up mind doesn't have to be loud. Sometimes it is steady. Sometimes it is patient. Sometimes it is choosing gentleness when everything in you wants to snap.

A made-up mind can build a business. But a made-up mind can also build a home.

Life Lesson #3: You Are Not Loved Because You Perform

I want my children to carry a love that is not tied to trophies or grades or achievements. The world will try to measure them. It will hand them scorecards and comparisons and expectations.

But in our home, they are not loved because they perform. They are loved because they belong.

That kind of love becomes a foundation. It gives a child courage to try. It gives them the safety to fail. It gives them the confidence to rise again.

And if I can give them that—truly give it to them—then I've already given them wealth.

The Fear I Rarely Admit

Here is one fear I don't say out loud often: I fear becoming a man my children respect but don't know.

It's possible to be admired from a distance. To be seen as "successful." To have a name, a reputation, a story. But fatherhood is not a biography. It is a relationship. And relationships are built in the small moments—bedtime prayers, car rides, kitchen table conversations, laughter on the porch, a hand on a shoulder.

I don't want to be a stranger in my own house.

I don't want my children to remember my voice as something they heard mostly through a closed office door.

That fear is holy to me. Not because it paralyzes me, but because it keeps me honest. It pulls me back when I drift too far into "build mode." It reminds me that the most important people in my life are not clients or partners or prospects. They are the ones who call me Dad.

A Father's Evening Reflection

Some evenings, when the Texas sun melts into the horizon and the world finally slows down, I watch my children move through the yard with the kind of freedom only kids have. Their laughter rises like a blessing. Their joy is simple, unforced, whole.

And I think about all the things I can't control. The economy. The industry. The storms that come for every man. The reality that no father can protect his children from everything.

But I can do this:

I can show them how to carry weight without dropping love. I can show them how to work without losing their soul. I can show them how to lead without becoming cold. I can show them how to rise without stepping on people. I can show them how to be strong and still be tender.

And in those quiet moments, I whisper a vow no one hears but God: Let me be steady. Let me be present. Let me be worthy of imitation. Let my example be louder than my ambition.

Because one day—long after the deals are forgotten and the titles are gone—my children won't remember my workload.

They will remember how I treated them when life was heavy.
And that is the legacy I am determined to leave.

Chapter 16 Balancing Ambition & Family

Ambition is a fire.

In the right place, it warms a home. In the wrong place, it burns one down.

Every man who dreams big must learn to walk a narrow edge — the place where purpose and family meet, where providing does not become replacing, and where success does not cost the very people you claim you are fighting for.

I learned that balance the hard way. And if I'm honest, I'm still learning it.

Because the truth is this: To rise without losing your family is the rarest victory a man can earn.

The Balance Didn't Begin With Freedom — It Began With Fatherhood

People assume my commitment to family began the day I left the captive world. They assume freedom of schedule created clarity of values.

But the truth is simpler — and harder.

That commitment began the moment I became a father.

Even in the old days — when quotas controlled every breath, when pressure never paused, when the company pulled me in every direction — I drew one line they could never cross.

My children would never grow up wondering if they came second. When each child was born, I took two or three weeks off. Not because I could afford it — I couldn't — but because I could not afford to miss those moments.

Management never understood.

"Two weeks, Steven? You'll fall behind." "You'll lose momentum." "You can't step away right now."

But I knew something they didn't.

The office could survive without me. My child's first days on earth would not wait.

So I walked away from spreadsheets. From ringing phones. From pending claims and performance metrics.

And I held my newborn. I memorized fingers. Counted breaths. Watched tiny chests rise and fall.

Those moments rewired something inside me.

The world teaches men to measure success in numbers. Fatherhood teaches a man to measure it in presence.

And that mindset never left me.

The Office That Helped Raise My Children

My children didn't grow up separated from my work.
They grew up inside it.
They crawled across office carpet before they could walk. They played under my desk while I typed notes. They sat on clients' laps. They watched me shake hands, listen carefully, and solve problems in real time.
And the highlight of my two oldest boys' childhood?
The shredder.

They still talk about it today — the thrill of "helping Dad at work," feeding stacks of old documents into the machine like they were partners instead of preschoolers.

Those moments weren't distractions. They were deposits.

Quiet deposits into what they believed a father should be.

They didn't see a man choosing work over family. They saw a man inviting his family into his work.

And I pray one day they realize why I worked so hard to build something worth inheriting.

The Weight of Pursuing a Dream When Your Spouse Can't See the Road Yet

But ambition — even the most noble kind — casts shadows.

There were nights my wife doubted what I was trying to build. Nights when my direction looked like chaos. Like a man chasing hope more than certainty.

She wasn't trying to cut me down. She was afraid.

Afraid of instability. Afraid of watching me fall again. Afraid of pouring everything into a dream that might never return the favor.

And when doubt comes from someone who loves you, it doesn't sound like criticism.

It sounds like fear wrapped in concern.

That kind of fear settles into your chest in a way no outside voice ever could.

Because ambition doesn't just demand courage from the dreamer. It demands faith from the family standing beside him.

The Beach Day That Burned a Lesson Into Me

There is one moment I still revisit — one that stings every time I replay it.

The year I left the captive world, something felt off. Leadership looked at me differently. The air had changed.

But I ignored the signs, hoping loyalty would cover the cracks.

That summer, I made a decision I regret to this day.

Instead of taking my usual two or three weeks, I cut our family vacation down to one week — just one — to "show commitment."

That week also happened to be district meeting week.

"Steven… are you sure you want to take that trip?" "This meeting is important to management."

I forced a smile.

"It's fine. I'll be at the meeting."

So on a day I should have been building sandcastles, chasing waves with my kids, and soaking in memories my family would remember forever…

I dressed up. Left the beach. And drove an hour and a half to a meeting room that cared nothing for the sacrifice it cost.

And how was I rewarded?

The Monday I returned — the very next business day — I was handed the ultimatum that opened the door to my exit.

Make your numbers… Or else.

That was the moment I learned a truth every man eventually faces.

A company will take every sacrifice you offer it and still let you go without hesitation.

But your family will feel every sacrifice you make — and love you anyway.

Never again.

Never again would I trade irreplaceable moments for approval. Never again would I place business above my home.

Fatherhood: The Commitment I Refuse to Break

Since leaving that world, I live by one immovable rule:

My family comes first — fully, fiercely, without apology.

I never miss games. Never miss programs. Never miss moments that matter.

My children know they can call me — and I will come.

And every Friday, we walk next door for ice cream.

Ten minutes where the world stops turning.

Success is sweet. But it has never tasted as sweet as those Fridays.

The Quiet War Inside Every Driven Man

There are nights I sit at my desk long after the house has gone quiet.

The lamp glows softly. The plans are unfinished.

And I ask myself:

Am I building something great — or something hollow? Will my children remember my presence — or my ambition? Will they know I worked for them — not away from them?

This is the war every driven man faces.

Ambition can lift a family out of struggle. Presence lifts a family into strength.

And so I choose presence. Again and again.

The Whisper That Keeps Me Anchored

Some nights, I step outside after the world goes quiet.

The porch light spills across the yard. Laughter echoes faintly in the air.

And I whisper the question that keeps me honest:

Will my children say they knew my heart?

Not my schedule. Not my stress. Not my pursuits.

My heart.

Because ambition without love is noise. Success without presence is emptiness. Legacy without family is a lonely monument.

So I pray:

"Lord, let me rise high… But never higher than the reach of my children's hands."

CHAPTER 17 Faith in the Seasons When No One Is Cheering

There are seasons in a man's life when momentum feels effortless—when phones ring, doors open, and encouragement flows freely. Those are the seasons people see. Those are the seasons people celebrate.

But there are other seasons.

Seasons when the phones go quiet. Seasons when effort outpaces results. Seasons when applause disappears. Seasons when even the people who once believed in you grow silent.

These are the seasons that test a man's faith—not faith in God alone, but faith in himself, his calling, and the path he has chosen.

I have learned that a man is not shaped in moments of recognition. He is shaped in moments of obscurity.

And the quiet seasons—when no one is cheering—are the most sacred classrooms of all.

The Silence That Follows the High

After the early momentum faded, I entered a stretch of days that felt eerily still. No dramatic collapse. No public failure. Just… quiet.

It is strange how silence can feel heavier than noise. Noise distracts. Silence confronts.

In that quiet, the mind becomes loud.

Questions surface that success once kept buried: Am I really good enough? Did I misread the calling? What if the early wins were luck? What if this is as far as I go?

These questions do not arrive like storms. They seep in like fog. Slow. Subtle. Persistent.

And if you are not careful, you begin to mistake the absence of applause for the absence of purpose.

But silence does not mean abandonment. It means preparation.

The Voices That Rise in the Dark

In the quiet seasons, voices emerge.

Some come from the past: You've failed before. You've been overlooked before. You've disappointed people before.

Others come from fear: What if you can't sustain this? What if this slows down permanently? What if the world moves on without you?

And then there is the most dangerous voice of all: The one that sounds like your own.

That voice questions your worth, your readiness, your strength. It pretends to be wisdom. It disguises itself as realism. But it is rooted in fear.

Yet alongside those voices—if you listen carefully—there is another. A quieter voice. A steadier one. One that does not shout, but anchors.

It says: Stand firm. You are not finished. This season is shaping you, not stopping you. Do not confuse silence with failure.

Faith is choosing which voice you obey when no one else is speaking.

The Discipline of Showing Up Unseen

When no one is watching, discipline becomes devotion.

In the quiet seasons, I learned to work without affirmation. To prepare without validation. To serve without recognition.

There were days I wondered if my effort mattered. Days when the work felt invisible. Days when progress seemed painfully slow.
But faith is not proven by outcomes alone. Faith is proven by consistency.
Showing up anyway. Preparing anyway. Serving anyway. Believing anyway.
This is where character is formed. Not in celebration—but in repetition.
I learned that faithfulness is not glamorous. It is quiet. It is routine. It is often boring. And it is powerful.
The Slow Growth Beneath the Surface
Farmers understand something the modern world has forgotten: Growth begins underground.
You cannot see roots forming. You cannot measure strength while it is building. You cannot rush the process without destroying the outcome.
In winter, fields look barren. But beneath the surface, preparation is happening.
The same is true in life.
Quiet seasons are not empty. They are fertile.
Skills deepen. Perspective sharpens. Patience matures. Ego softens. Purpose clarifies.
Looking back, I can see now that God was doing more in those silent months than He ever did in the loud ones.
He was refining me. Removing shortcuts. Stripping away identity built on performance. Teaching me to stand without applause.
The Small Miracles That Sustain Faith
Faith is often sustained not by miracles—but by moments.
A kind text. A referral that arrives unexpectedly. A client who remembers how you treated them. A conversation that restores perspective. A calm moment at the end of a long day.
These are not headlines. They are lifelines.

When I stopped looking for dramatic confirmation, I began noticing quiet provision. Enough strength for today. Enough clarity for the next step. Enough peace to continue.

Faith grows when you learn to recognize provision without spectacle.

When the World Goes Quiet, God Gets Clear

In loud seasons, it is easy to confuse momentum with calling. In quiet seasons, calling becomes unmistakable.

When the noise faded, I could finally hear what mattered. I could evaluate my motives. Clarify my priorities. Recenter my values.

I learned that my worth was not tied to production. That my identity was not dependent on results. That my calling did not require validation.

Faith deepened because it had to. There was nothing else to lean on. No applause. No affirmation. Just obedience.

The Strength Born in Solitude

There is a strength that can only be built in solitude.

It is the strength of a man who no longer needs approval. The confidence of someone who knows why he stands. The steadiness of a person who has already faced doubt and survived.

Once you endure a season without applause, you gain something permanent: Freedom.

Freedom from chasing recognition. Freedom from external validation. Freedom to build at your own pace.

You stop performing. You start becoming.

The Day I Realized I Was Stronger

One evening, after a long stretch of quiet effort, I realized something profound: I was still standing.

Not celebrated. Not praised. But steady.

I had not quit. I had not compromised. I had not abandoned the calling.

That realization mattered more than any recognition ever could.

Because if I could stand without applause, I could stand through anything.

The Season That Crowned Me

Looking back now, I understand:

The season when no one was cheering was not punishment. It was preparation.

It crowned me with resilience. It anchored my faith. It clarified my identity.

Success may return. Momentum may rise again.

But the strength built in silence remains.

And now, when applause comes—or doesn't—I am unchanged.

Because I no longer rise for recognition. I rise because it is who I am.

And if you are in a season where no one is cheering, know this:

You are not behind. You are not forgotten. You are not failing.

You are being formed.

And when the season shifts—as it always does—you will stand taller, steadier, and stronger than ever before.

Not because the world applauded you. But because you learned to rise without it.

CHAPTER 18 Building Wiatrek Group at City Centre Insurance

When June arrived, it didn't ask permission. It didn't creep in politely or ease its way into my life. It
came the way South Texas summer always comes—thick heat rising from black clay, cicadas tuning
their evening chorus, sunlight stretching endlessly across U.S. Highway 181 until the whole world felt
dipped in gold.
June carried a message I could feel before I could explain it:
Rise. This is the month things begin to turn.
For months, I had been working in silence—learning, building, stumbling, enduring. No
announcements. No grand openings. No applause. No one handing me a trophy for staying in the
fight. Just discipline. Just faith. Just the daily decision to show up when quitting would have been
easier and comfort would have been convenient.
But June was different.

June was the first month the ground beneath my feet stopped trembling and began to feel solid. The first month where "survival" started to loosen its grip and "purpose" started to take its place. Not everything was perfect—nothing about starting over is perfect—but because the work finally

started to feel true. The systems began to make sense. The phone began to ring with something

other than worry. The relationships started to stack one on top of another like bricks.

And one brick at a time, Wiatrek Group began to look like a real foundation instead of a hopeful idea.

The Office That Became a Beginning

My small office inside the REMAX building sat on a porch overlooking Highway 181—a steady river of

ranch trucks, oilfield pickups, commuters, and farm rigs rolling north toward San Antonio or south into

Karnes County. It wasn't a skyscraper. It wasn't a marble lobby. It wasn't a corporate headquarters

with an elevator and a badge reader. It was a simple space, tucked into a place where people still do

business face to face and still believe a handshake means something. Each morning before unlocking the door, I paused at the window and watched the traffic move. That

motion grounded me. No matter what storm a man carries internally, the world keeps going—parents

driving children to school, workers heading to job sites, farmers hauling feed, lives unfolding one mile

at a time. In that steady flow of headlights and dust, I felt a quiet reminder: you can be hurting and still

keep moving. You can be uncertain and still take the next step.

Outside, gravel crunched beneath boots as people climbed the porch steps. Inside, the air was cool,
the lights warm, and the quiet electricity of something new being born filled the room. It wasn't
glamorous. It wasn't polished. But it was ours. More importantly—it was mine.
My first headquarters. My first true space as an independent agency owner. The birthplace of a
legacy I prayed would outlive me.
There were mornings I sat at that desk early, coffee in hand, a legal pad filled with handwritten
notes—renewals to review, carriers to call, quotes to follow up on, people to serve. And I'd feel the weight of it. Not the old weight of quotas and fear—the kind that crushes a man—but a different weight. A sacred one. The weight of ownership. The weight of being responsible for the outcome. The weight of knowing that if this thing was going to live, it would live because I kept breathing life into it. That kind of responsibility does something to a man. It doesn't just test his work ethic. It tests his character.

The Team That Found Its Rhythm

By June, my team began to move as one.
My first producer—young, hungry, determined—started finding his confidence. I saw it in his posture.
Heard it in his voice. Felt it in the way he approached challenges with less fear and more ownership.
At first, he had looked like most new producers look—eager but unsure, trying to be helpful without
getting in the way, learning the language of carriers and underwriting and risk. But June did what

June always does for a growing man: it brought heat. And heat refines. He started asking better questions. He started spotting problems before they became fires. He
started sounding like someone who belonged in this profession—not because he memorized a script, but because he was beginning to understand the heart behind the work.
And then there was my mother.
A woman who had already lived a full career and already earned her rest, yet chose to step out of
retirement to stand beside me. Her presence brought a steadiness no training manual could ever
teach. She treated every client with dignity. She organized the office with care. She softened the hard
edges of my stress simply by being in the room.
Seeing her seated at a desk inside my agency—helping build something born from my lowest
season—did more for my confidence than she will probably ever know.
There's something humbling about having your mother in your business. She doesn't care about your titles. She doesn't care about your ego. She cares about your integrity, your effort, and whether you're doing right by people. When she looked at me, she didn't see an "agency owner." She saw her son—the same boy she raised—still trying to prove he could build something good. And in her quiet presence, I felt a kind of validation you can't buy: the belief of someone who knows your whole story and still chooses to stand with you.

Momentum That Cannot Be Bought

June was the month unseen effort began to show itself.

Phones rang more often. Quotes turned into policies. Policies turned into relationships. Relationships turned into trust. And all of it happened without a marketing budget. No ads. No billboards. No mailers. No gimmicks.

Everything grew through word of mouth—through how people felt after speaking with us.

We weren't selling policies. We were earning trust.

In small towns, people don't just shop price. They shop character. They shop reputation. They shop

the feeling they get when they sit across from you and you look them in the eye like they matter. They

can tell if you're listening for their story—or listening for your commission.

Where competitors hid behind scripts and defended rate increases like trained parrots, I chose a

different path:

Listen first. Relate second. Acknowledge fear. Tell the truth. Respect dignity. Guide with honesty.

There were days clients walked in frustrated, already braced for battle. They'd sit down and start with the same line I'd heard a thousand times:

"Steven, I don't understand why it went up again."

And I'd let them finish. I'd let them vent. Sometimes I'd let them cuss. Because when people are

scared, they don't need to be corrected—they need to be heard. And then, when the storm of

emotion softened, I'd say what most people never hear from an agent: "Before we do anything, tell me what you want your insurance to accomplish."

That question changes the room.

Because suddenly it's not about a premium. It's about a family. A home. A truck that gets a man to work. A small business that feeds kids. A farm that has been in the family longer than a mortgage ever could explain.

Then I'd tell them the truth gently:

"Yes, rates increased. They may rise again someday. We can shop it. We can adjust it. But every

choice has trade-offs. My job isn't to pressure you. My job is to make sure you understand what

you're choosing—and why."

And I'd end the way my grandfather taught me to live: plain, honest, and respectful.

"You're the one holding the steering wheel. I'm just helping you see the road."

I didn't do anything miraculous. I simply treated people the way my father treated everyone—with sincerity and respect. Humanity became our advantage. And humanity still wins—especially in a world that has forgotten it.

A June Afternoon That Changed Everything

One warm afternoon, after finishing a long conversation with a client, I stepped onto the porch to

breathe.

Highway 181 hummed below, tires singing against asphalt. Cars moved north and south, each one carrying someone's story, someone's burden, someone's hope. The sun sat high and bright. The air carried that particular South Texas mix—dust and heat and the faint sweetness of summer fields.

Behind me, through the office window, I saw my mother helping a client and my producer working through a quote. The glow of purpose filled that small space. And something rose in my chest—quiet, unexpected, undeniable:

We're doing this.

We're really doing this.

Not by accident. Not by luck. Not by shortcuts.

But by faith, effort, and the refusal to quit when quitting would have been easier.

The man who once doubted his worth now stood on the porch of his own agency, watching

something worthy of the family name take shape. For a moment, I saw my story from outside. The cardboard box. The fear. The silence. The long nights where the only thing keeping me upright was the belief that God doesn't waste a man's pain.

And I realized something that hit me like a blessing:

This wasn't just a business.

This was restoration.

June's Benediction

As the sun lowered that evening, the sky washed itself in deep oranges and reds. I rested my hands on the porch rail, feeling the warmth of the wood beneath my palms. The heat of the day began to break, and a gentle breeze rolled through town like mercy.
June had restored me. It was the month survival gave way to purpose.
The month Wiatrek Group
stepped out of reaction mode and into calling.
I bowed my head slightly and whispered the same prayer my ancestors must have spoken over fields of crops and acres of hope:
Thank You for bringing me this far.
Thank You for this ground beneath my feet.
And thank You for letting me build again.
Then I turned, opened the office door, and stepped back inside—into the hum of work, the warmth of purpose, and the future God had prepared long before I knew to ask.
June had arrived. And with it, the beginning of everything.

Part V – Building the New Life

The best way to find yourself is to lose yourself in the service of others.

               Mahatma Gandhi

CHAPTER 19 Scaling Wiatrek Group: The Unexpected Acceleration

June arrived not with fireworks, but with a quiet momentum I didn't see coming.

And in this business — in any business — quiet momentum is often the most powerful kind.

By the time June arrived, I was still working remotely — just like my agents. My office was wherever I could set my laptop down: the kitchen table, a quiet corner of the house, sometimes the front seat of my truck between appointments. Phones rang, policies were written, decisions were made — all without walls, signage, or a physical place to call our own.

Independence had given us freedom.

It had not yet given us roots.

That changed on June 1.

When I unlocked the door to our office for the first time, it wasn't just a change of address. It was a shift in identity. Wiatrek Group was no longer an idea operating out of borrowed space — it was becoming something real.

There were no announcements. No ribbon cuttings. No victory laps. No dramatic turning point anyone could point to and say, "That's when it all changed." There was only a subtle shift in the air — the kind you don't notice until you stop long enough to breathe.

The office sat beside a small coffee shop, its daily rhythm blending quietly with my own. The gravel lot had only just begun to feel familiar beneath my boots. The desk was still new. The walls still bare. My second agent — my mother — was still finding her rhythm, learning the systems, learning how independence feels different when it carries real responsibility.

And I was still learning how to breathe in this new world without the weight of fear pressing on my chest.

Fear has a way of lingering even after you've escaped the thing that caused it.

For months, I had lived in survival mode. Every decision carried weight. Every phone call mattered. Every mistake felt amplified. Independence had stripped away the safety net. There was no corporate buffer anymore. No one else to absorb the consequences. Every win and every failure stopped at my name.

But something was changing.

The long months of foundation-laying, late-night work, and unseen battles had planted seeds I didn't even realize were growing. I had been so focused on doing the next right thing — keeping promises, returning calls, protecting families — that I hadn't stopped to notice what persistence was quietly producing.

And now, in ways that felt both humbling and surreal, those seeds began to sprout.

Not cautiously. Not tentatively.

But unmistakably.

A Network Rekindled — One Door at a Time

It started, as many meaningful things do, with a simple phone call.

A local realtor — a woman I respected, admired, and had once helped with a policy no one else in town could offer — reached out unexpectedly. Her voice carried a genuine excitement, the kind that doesn't come from obligation or salesmanship.

"Steven," she said, "I think we'd make a great team. I'd love to collaborate if you're willing."

Her REMAX office sat right beside the coffee shop. When I walked in, something inside me settled. There was no tension in the room. No guarded conversations. No posturing about territory or advantage.

It felt right. It felt natural. It felt like the kind of abundance-minded partnership small towns rarely get — but desperately need.

We talked about clients. About families. About how many people fall through the cracks when professionals operate in silos instead of community. We talked about trust — how it's built face to face, over time, through consistency rather than contracts.

And without formalities, ultimatums, or ego, we agreed to collaborate. Just like that, my first true office space was born.

She probably doesn't realize this, but that simple, gracious act of partnership became one of the greatest blessings of my early journey. It reminded me that not everyone operates from scarcity. Not everyone guards opportunity like it's a finite resource.

Some people still believe in opening doors rather than locking them. And in a quiet twist of irony, she eventually filled the seat on the Economic Development Corporation board I had once vacated — a board I stepped away from after growing weary of closed-handed thinking and short-sighted leadership.

Life has a way of placing people where they're needed most.

The Momentum No One Warned Me About

Word began to spread — not because I advertised, but because I served.

I didn't have billboards. I didn't run flashy campaigns. I didn't promise anything I couldn't personally deliver.

I simply showed up. Answered the phone. Asked better questions. Stayed longer than expected.

And then the acceleration began.

Local realtors started calling. Commercial realtors from San Antonio reached out. Lenders, builders, and business owners asked for introductions.

Over and over, I heard the same phrase in different voices:

"We've been waiting for someone who actually listens."

Then came the surprise I never expected.

Men from my previous life — car salesmen I had worked alongside years earlier — began tracking me down.

"Steven, can you still help our customers?" "We've missed the way you took care of people." "No one does it the way you did."

Standing there, absorbing those words, I realized something that reshaped the way I saw my past.

My value had never been borrowed from a company name. It had never been assigned by a title. It had never been dependent on a logo. My value was built. Built through consistency.

Built through follow-through. Built through years of doing right by people when no one was watching.

When Expertise Finds Its Voice

My first group health policy wasn't massive in size, but within our firm, it was historic — the first to be issued. It represented more than premium or commission. It represented credibility.

Suddenly, I wasn't just learning. I was contributing.

I was the one people asked questions to. The one others reached out to for clarity. The one leadership pointed to when they said, "This is what early-stage success looks like."

Then came the farm and ranch calls.
Even though our firm didn't yet have a defined farm and ranch
market, agents kept reaching out.
"Steven, how would you write this?" "What exposures should I be
looking for here?" "What questions do I need to ask before binding?"
Those conversations pulled me back to my roots. Back to the land.
Back to the environments that shaped my instincts long before I ever
knew what underwriting meant.
For the first time since stepping into independence, I felt that old
confidence returning — not the hollow confidence built on quotas or
titles, but the steady kind earned through lived experience.
Confidence grounded in competence. Confidence anchored in truth.

The Power of Returning Voices

Then something even sweeter began to happen.
Messages came in from former captive agents.
Men and women I once viewed as equals — and some I once viewed
as mentors.
They reached out not with ego, but with humility.
"Hey Steven… can I run something by you?" "Your advice really
helped me last time." "You've become a builder — and I respect that."
We began collaborating instead of competing. Sharing ideas. Referring
clients. Learning from one another instead of guarding information
like currency.
That's when I realized I was no longer just an agent.
Not because of a title. Not because of a plaque. Not because anyone
declared it so.
But because people were trusting me with their questions, their clients,
their challenges.
Leadership is never taken. It is earned — slowly, quietly, through
consistency and heart.

A Windfall of Gratitude I Never Saw Coming

As June unfolded, doors seemed to open faster than I could walk
through them.
Some afternoons I would sit at my desk, hands resting on the
keyboard, and feel gratitude settle over me like a warm blanket. This
wasn't supposed to happen this fast. I wasn't supposed to feel this
supported so early.
But every referral, every compliment, every returned relationship
whispered the same truth:
People weren't coming back for policies. They were coming back for
trust.
Trust is slow to build. Easy to lose. And rare to find.
Somehow, through years of listening, serving, and staying present, I
had built something far more valuable than I ever realized — a
reputation that outlived the company logo that once hung above my
door.

Standing at the Edge of What's Next

When the day finally settled and the office grew quiet, I stepped onto
the small porch outside my door. The gravel lot stretched beneath me.
Highway 181 hummed steadily into the South Texas night.
Cars rolled past in an unbroken line, each pair of headlights carving a
brief path through the darkness. I stood there watching them — not as
a man defeated by his past, but as a man witnessing the first true signs
of his rise.
For months, I had questioned everything. Wondered if anyone would
follow me. Feared I had been forgotten. Feared the world would move
on without me.
But tonight, the evidence spoke differently.

Realtors returning. Car salesmen calling. Agents seeking guidance.
Opportunities unfolding with grace and momentum.
This acceleration wasn't accidental.
It was the harvest of years spent doing right by people when no one
was watching.
No shortcuts. No scripts. No manipulation.
Just sincerity. Just service. Just heart.
I breathed in the warm summer air and whispered into the night,
"Lord… thank You. I'm ready for whatever comes next."
Then I turned off the porch light, locked the door, and walked into the
darkness with a steady heart and a quiet certainty.
I wasn't just building Wiatrek Group.
I was becoming the kind of man capable of leading it into the future.

Chapter 20 Becoming the Agent You Always Wanted to Be and Becoming the Face of Your Community

There comes a time in a man's life when he finally understands that he was never just building a career… he was building himself.
Not in the ways the world applauds. Not through titles or trophies or polished résumés. But through pressure. Through patience. Through perseverance no one else ever sees.
Every setback. Every silent season. Every triumph that went unnoticed. Every night he went to bed uncertain of tomorrow.
All of it was shaping his character — not his résumé.
That realization doesn't arrive all at once. It comes quietly, often after the storms have passed, when a man finally has the space to reflect on who he has become beneath the grind.
Somewhere along my journey, sometime after rising from the ashes of the captive world and stepping into the freedom of independence, I realized a truth that humbled me:
I had become the kind of agent I once wished existed.
Not perfect. Not polished. Not corporate-made. But real. Grounded. Empathetic. Trustworthy.

The kind of professional I searched for years ago — not with sophistication, but with sincerity. Someone who would slow down when the world rushed. Someone who would tell the truth even when it wasn't convenient. Someone whose presence felt steady instead of transactional.

Because the greatest secret of this entire profession — the one the corporate world never taught — is this:

Insurance is not the business of selling policies.

Insurance is the business of selling trust.

A policy is paperwork. Premiums are math. Coverage limits are words in ink.

But trust… Trust is sacred.

Trust is earned in late-night conversations and difficult truths. Trust is built when you listen longer than you speak. Trust is formed when a client realizes you're not there to extract money… you're there to protect their life.

And trust, I eventually realized, is what they were buying from me all along.

The Art of Listening — And the Ministry Hidden Within It

Clients venting about rates taught me more about humanity than any conference or training class ever did.

They didn't need scripts. They didn't need rehearsed explanations.

They didn't need to be "handled."

They needed sincerity.

They needed someone who didn't rush them. Someone who didn't defend the company like a corporate soldier. Someone who didn't talk down to them or minimize their worry.

They needed someone who said, "I hear you. And you're not wrong — this is hard."

And in those moments, I realized something profound:

Listening — truly listening — is one of the highest forms of service.

It is a ministry in its own right.

Those conversations weren't about insurance. They were about being human together.

Fear has a way of disguising itself as anger. Confusion often masks grief. And frustration usually comes from feeling unheard.

When people feel listened to, something changes. Anger dissolves. Fear softens. Trust takes root.

I learned that no policy explanation carries more power than presence. No script is more effective than patience. And no closing technique compares to a man who genuinely cares.

Stepping Into the Role My Community Needed

I never set out to become "the face of my community."

That kind of role isn't something you claim. In small towns, leadership is never appointed — it is recognized.

As a city councilman, as a neighbor, as a business owner, as a father — I found that my life was intertwined with every person who walked through my door.

Their kids played with mine. Their parents sat in the same pews. Their livelihoods rose and fell with the same local economy.

People began to look to me not because of a title, but because they saw someone who showed up.

Someone steady. Someone who told the truth kindly. Someone who served without a spotlight.

And I began to understand something most leadership books miss: Small towns do not elevate the loudest. They elevate the most faithful. Those who stand firm when it would be easier to fold. Those who pour into others when no one is counting. Those who choose character over convenience.

Reputation isn't built through announcements. It's built through consistency.

Learning to Serve Without Taking — The Knights of Columbus Lesson

One of the most humbling tests of who I had become came from a place of faith, not business.

As a member of the Knights of Columbus, our council occasionally meets with K of C insurance representatives. Good men. Hard-working men. Trying to serve their flock just as I serve mine.

What surprised me was what happened after those meetings.

The next day, my phone would ring.

"Steven, can you look over this?" "Steven, does this make sense to you?" "Steven, would you buy this?" "Steven, what would you recommend?"

The old version of me — the one shaped by quotas, pressure, scarcity — might have seen this as an opportunity to swoop in and rewrite their policies.

But that man is gone.

Today, I do something different. Something that honors my faith and my community more than any commission ever could.

I review their policies. I validate their concerns. I offer questions to help them think clearly. I explain what is fair, what is good, what is reasonable. I give them the full truth without agenda.

And then I tell them:

"If you trust the Knights' representative, stay with him. My role is not to take — my role is to guide."

Because leadership, I've learned, is not about winning business. It is about winning respect.

And respect is only won when a man chooses integrity over opportunity.

In those conversations, something crystallized for me:

A man becomes worthy of trust when he refuses to take advantage of it.

Two Roles Becoming One: Agent and Advocate

My life in insurance and my life in public service began to overlap in ways I never expected.

The values that made me a good agent were the same values that made me a good councilman.

Empathy. Honesty. Consistency. Patience. Integrity. A willingness to do the right thing even when no one is watching.

Leadership began to change shape in my mind — not as a ladder to climb, but as a burden to carry with dignity.

Because when people trust you with their families, their livelihoods, and their future, the weight is real. You feel it in the decisions you make and the words you choose. You carry it home at night.

And as my agency grew, as my reputation grew, as my roots deepened further into this community I love — I finally understood what all the hardship had been preparing me for:

To become a man my community could count on.

A man who protects. A man who listens. A man who leads without asking for applause. A man whose handshake still means something.

Becoming the Man Your Community Sees When They Speak Your Name

Some evenings, when I close up my office and the last rays of sun settle over Highway 181, I stand on the porch and watch cars drift by. Families heading home. Farm trucks coated in dust. Parents tired from work but grateful for another day.

And I think about legacy — not the kind written on plaques, but the kind whispered in conversations when your name comes up.

Because one day, people won't remember the policies I sold. They won't remember the premiums I quoted. They won't remember the numbers.

But they will remember how I treated them. They will remember whether I listened. They will remember whether I stood firm. They will remember whether I served them well.

And if my name is spoken with respect, if my children inherit a reputation built on integrity, if my community knows I tried to do right by them —

Then I will know I became the agent… and the man… I always hoped to be.

Chapter 21 Writing My First Book

There comes a moment in every man's journey when success alone no longer satisfies the soul.

It is a strange moment, because on the surface everything appears right. The numbers are improving. The phone is ringing. The problems that once kept you awake at night have softened, at least enough to let you breathe again. From the outside, it looks like arrival. Even as Wiatrek Group @ City Centre Insurance was growing, even as policies were being written, even as momentum was building faster than anything I had dared to dream… something inside me still felt unsteady.

Not broken—no, those pieces had already been put back together— but hollow, like a room missing its most important furniture. Functional, but incomplete. Standing, but unsettled.

My agency was thriving. My clients trusted me. My producers were growing. My community embraced me again.

And yet…

There was an emptiness in me I could not ignore. A quiet ache. A whisper in the dark.

I had rebuilt my business… but I had not fully rebuilt myself.

That realization was uncomfortable. It challenged the idea that success alone could heal what had been wounded. It forced me to confront the truth that restoration is not the same thing as transformation.
Over those months, as I met more agency owners and reconnected with former captive agents who had walked the same lonely road I once feared, I began to see something I had never fully acknowledged before:
This side of the industry can be astonishingly lonely.
Independent doesn't just describe the agency model—it describes the man himself.
No team meetings. No water cooler conversations. No hallway coaching. Just you, your desk, your decisions, your doubts.
Freedom, yes. But also silence.
And silence has a way of amplifying unresolved questions.
But at City Centre Insurance, something different happened.
It wasn't just a company—it was a network of lives, stories, and struggles overlapping in ways that felt strangely familiar and unexpectedly comforting. Men who had lost titles but not integrity. Men rebuilding families while rebuilding careers. Men who understood that success meant nothing if it cost you your soul.
And that's when it began.
Not with a plan. Not with a dream. Not with ambition.
But with a single conversation.
"You Should Write a Book…"
One evening after a long day of meetings and laughter and shared struggles at HQ, I found myself talking with José, a fellow agency owner with a sharp mind and a humble spirit.
He said casually—almost jokingly, but not quite:
"You know, Steven… we applied one of your ideas today. It helped our new producers. Man, you should really write a book."
It landed softly—but it stayed.

At first, I dismissed it. I wasn't an author. I wasn't trained in writing. I was an insurance agent who had only recently found solid footing again.

But a few months later, at another gathering, a different agency owner leaned in and said:

"Your advice has helped my team. Seriously—you should write a book."

This time the words didn't land softly.

This time they struck something deep—the place inside me that had once been bruised, once been silenced, once believed it had nothing left to offer.

The place that whispered:

Maybe your story matters more than you think.

The Four-Hour Drive Home — Where the Decision Was Made

(Northwest on I-10 → Lytle → Nixon → Stockdale → Poth)

That night, after the meeting, I climbed into my truck and began the long journey home. I merged onto Interstate 10, heading northwest, the sky unfolding into a dark canvas dotted with stars that had watched generations of men wrestle with calling and purpose.

The city lights receded. The road opened wide. And somewhere between the hum of the tires and the rhythm of my breathing, the thought returned:

Write a book…

By the time I reached Lytle, the interstate had given way to FM roads wrapped in quiet fields and country dark. The kind of dark that doesn't frighten you—the kind that invites honesty.

From Lytle to Nixon, memories surfaced like mile markers.

Agents who had quit. Agents who had fallen. Agents who had been abandoned by their companies. Agents who had never been told their worth.

Men who believed failure had disqualified them.

And I wondered:

How many could stand again if someone just handed them a map?

By Stockdale, the road narrowed—and so did my doubts.

I began to realize the truth I had avoided for years:

I had been given insight, experience, wounds, victories, and wisdom—not to hoard, but to share.

The final stretch into Poth felt almost sacred. My hometown lights glowed softly against the night, as if welcoming a man walking toward a new calling.

When I turned into my driveway, I stepped out of the truck not asking:

Should I write a book?

But declaring:

It's time to write it.

The Hardest Journey Wasn't the Writing… It Was the Remembering

The moment I began typing, I realized the truth:

Writing a book was not going to be a celebration—it was going to be surgery.

To write honestly, I had to revisit memories I had locked away. The humiliation. The fear. The nights I felt like a failure. The shame I carried home in a cardboard box. The mornings I woke up unemployed and terrified.

Every chapter forced me to face a version of myself I had prayed I would never meet again.

But something unexpected happened.

The more I wrote, the more I healed.

Each word felt like a stitch, closing wounds I had learned to live with but never truly addressed. The ache in my soul—the one I couldn't name, the one I couldn't shake—began to soften.

For the first time since leaving the captive world, I felt whole.

Not because writing erased the pain, but because writing redeemed it.

Healing Through Service

What surprised me most wasn't the writing—it was what happened as I wrote.

I felt humbled.

Truly humbled.

Because I realized that everything I had endured—every wound, every setback, every fear—was preparing me to help others climb out of the same darkness.

For the first time in my career, I wasn't just selling insurance. I wasn't just building an agency.

I was reaching back, with a hand extended, to the next man walking through fire.

And that filled the hollow place inside me with a purpose I didn't know I needed.

The Book That Rebuilt the Man

Late one night, hands resting on the keyboard, the house quiet and the world still, I sat alone in the glow of a small desk lamp and realized something profound:

I wasn't writing a book.

I was becoming the man who could write one.

The pain had shaped me. The silence had stretched me. The healing had steadied me. The calling had claimed me.

And as I listened to the distant hum of the night and felt the warmth of the lamp on my hands, I whispered to myself—almost as a prayer: Maybe this book wasn't meant to make me successful. Maybe it was meant to make me whole.

That night, I closed my laptop, looked up with grateful tears in my eyes, and finally understood:

The story I had been running from had become the story that would lead others home.

And in telling it, I had come home too.

Chapter 22 Becoming "Steven Wiatrek, Author"

The unexpected shift from small-town agent to someone people began
looking toward

I never imagined the word author would one day sit beside my name.
That title belonged to people whose lives seemed bigger, whose voices
carried farther, whose stories felt destined to be told long before they
ever put pen to paper. Authors, in my mind, were born with
permission — permission to speak, to teach, to be heard.
Not a small-town kid from Poth. Not a farm-raised boy from
Kosciusko. Not the son of humble, hard-working parents who taught
me that storytelling happened around a kitchen table — not between
printed pages.
In my world, stories were passed down over coffee cups and tailgates.
They were told between chores and church, between planting and
harvest. They were lived first and spoken later, rarely written down
because life itself carried the lesson.
So the day my book was published, I didn't feel like I had crossed into
a new category of humanity.
I felt something quieter. Deeper. Truer.
I felt seen in a way I never had before — not seen as impressive or
important, but seen as understood. As if the road I had walked, with

all its failures and rebuilding, had finally formed a shape others could recognize.

The People Who Knew Me "Before" Were the First to Notice

Before the strangers. Before the industry. Before the bookstores and online listings.

It was former classmates — people who once sat beside me in cramped Poth classrooms, people who ran the same hallways and lived the same small-town rhythm.

Their messages came fast.

"Man… YOU wrote a book?" "I'm proud of you, brother." "Look at you… doing what none of us expected."

It felt surreal.

Not because they were impressed — but because people who knew the earliest version of me were recognizing the newest version of me. There is nothing as grounding as being acknowledged by those who knew you when you were just another kid in tennis shoes, eating cafeteria pizza, dreaming the small, local dreams of a small, local life. They remembered me before ambition ever took shape. Before responsibility sharpened my edges. Before hardship taught me who I was going to be when things fell apart.

And somehow, they could see that the boy they knew had grown — not into someone else — but into himself.

Family Pride — The Kind That Carries the Weight of Generations

Then came messages from my aunts, uncles, and cousins — family scattered across South Texas who had watched my journey quietly from afar.

They told me they bought the book. They told me they were proud. They told me I was doing something no one in our family had ever done.

Their pride carried a different weight — the weight of legacy.

On both sides of my family, people worked the land, raised livestock, served their churches, survived droughts, depressions, wars, and lean years. They built communities with their hands, not their headlines. So when they said, "We're proud of you, Steven," it felt like I was carrying them forward — one sentence at a time. Honoring their sacrifices with something new that still grew from the same soil that raised them.

A Librarian's Shock — and a Full-Circle Moment

One afternoon, I ran into a familiar figure from my high school days — not a teacher, but my school librarian.

The woman who watched over countless generations of students. Who placed books in the hands of kids who never knew how much they needed them. Who fostered curiosity long before we understood its power.

When she heard I had become a published author, she didn't speak at first. She simply studied me — as if comparing the boy she remembered with the man standing before her.

Then she shook her head softly and smiled.

"Steven… you wrote a book. You really did it."

In her eyes I saw something I hadn't expected — pride, yes, but also recognition.

Recognition that the outspoken kid with too much energy and too many opinions had done something rare. He had turned life into story. Pain into purpose. Experience into wisdom.

That moment humbled me more than any review ever could.

Inspiring Others — Without Ever Intending To

Then came the comments I never saw coming.

"You inspired me to start writing." "You made me believe my story matters too." "You gave me courage to chase something I've buried for years."

I never wrote to impress. I never wrote to be admired. I wrote because
I felt a pull to serve — the same pull that guides me in insurance,
leadership, and community.

Somehow, quietly, unknowingly, the book had become a lantern for
others. Not a spotlight. Not a fireworks show. A lantern — steady,
gentle, guiding.

The Chuckles — The Affectionate Kind Only Small Towns Give

Of course, in Poth and Kosciusko, humility is baked into the soil.

"You wrote a book? Boy, you're crazy."

And I always smiled, because that's how my community speaks love
— with humor, teasing, and a pat on the back disguised as a jab.

My response became a running joke.

"Crazy like a fox."

A fox isn't crazy at all. It's clever. It adapts. It survives. It thrives
quietly — exactly how this journey unfolded.

The Quiet Monday Afternoon That Changed Nothing — and
Everything

There was no party. No celebration. No confetti.

Just me sitting alone in my small office on a quiet Monday afternoon,
sunlight washing across my desk, the hum of Highway 181 drifting
through the window.

When I clicked "publish," there was no thunder, no cinematic
moment. But inside me, something settled — something steady and
unshakable.

I didn't feel bigger. I didn't feel famous. I didn't feel transformed.

I felt aligned.

For the first time, my inner voice and my outer life were telling the
same story.

The Quiet Becoming

Later that evening, I stepped onto my porch and watched the slow
river of cars drift down Highway 181.

People heading home. People heading to work. People moving through their lives with no idea that a man behind a gravel lot had crossed a private milestone.

And as the wind brushed across my face, I knew the truth.

Becoming an author didn't make me different. It made me more myself.

It awakened the storyteller in my blood. The teacher in my spirit. The servant in my heart.

And as the sun lowered over South Texas, I whispered a promise to the open sky.

If my words can help even one person rise, then everything I've lived — every fall, every bruise, every season of silence — was worth it.

Because that is what authors truly are: servants of stories, keepers of lessons, lanterns in the dark.

And on that quiet Monday afternoon, I became one.

Part VI – Letters to My Children

The greatest legacy one can pass on to one's children is not money or possessions, but rather a legacy of character and faith.
    Billy Graham

Letter 1 To My Children: Be Brave Enough to Chase Your Ambitions (Even If It Means Starting Over)

My dear children,

There will come a day — sooner than you think — when life will place a choice before you.

A crossroads. A moment where the ground beneath your feet feels fragile, and the path ahead feels uncertain. A moment when staying where you are feels safe... but stepping forward feels necessary.

That moment will not arrive with fanfare. It will come quietly. Disguised as discomfort. Whispering instead of shouting.

In that sacred moment, my prayer for you is simple:

Be brave enough to chase your ambitions... even if it means starting over.

Starting over is not failure. It is the purest form of faith a human being can live.

It is the moment you decide that obedience matters more than comfort, and integrity matters more than fear.

I know this because I have lived it.

When I Started Over — And What It Cost Me

You were all too young to understand the season your father walked through, though one day you will read about it in the chapters that came before this one.

You will feel the weight of those words — the fear, the doubt, the pressure, the silence — but you will never fully know how heavy it truly was.

And thank God for that.

There were days when I felt like a cracked vessel still trying to carry water. Days when I questioned whether I had anything left worth giving. Days when starting over felt less like renewal and more like punishment.

There were mornings I woke up already exhausted. Nights I lay awake wondering how a man rebuilds when the world seems to have already passed judgment.

But I did it anyway.

I did it because of you.

Because I never wanted you to grow up believing that a man must stay where he is tolerated instead of going where he can thrive. I never wanted you to believe that stability mattered more than dignity. Or that fear should ever have the final word in your story.

Starting over is frightening.

But it is far more frightening to wake up one day and realize you stayed small because you were too afraid to see how big your life could have become.

You Will Not Walk the Same Road I Did — But You Will Walk Your Own

I cannot shield you from hardship. I cannot promise your path will be smooth. I cannot stop disappointment from reaching you — nor would I, even if I could.

Because hardship is not your enemy.

Hardship is the anvil on which courage is forged.

Every seed must break before it grows. Every warrior must bleed before he becomes strong. Every life worth living must shed its old skin before stepping into the new.

When your moment comes — when God whispers that it is time to rise, to trust, to leap —

I pray you listen.

Not to the fear. Not to the noise. Not to the voices that say you are crazy, unqualified, unprepared, or unworthy.

Listen to the quiet truth inside you — the one that flickers like a flame but never goes out:

"There is more in you than you know."

I saw that truth in each of you the moment you were placed in my arms.

You Were Never Meant for Small Lives

Let me tell you something you may not understand until you are grown:

Your father pushed you because he believed in you.

Not because I wanted perfection. Not because I wanted you to become who I never was. But because I saw greatness in you long before you could see it for yourself.

Yes, I was strict at times. Yes, I pushed you to try harder, climb higher, take responsibility, show respect, and expect more from yourselves.

And I know there were days you resented it.

But hear this truth clearly, without bitterness or doubt:

I pushed you because I saw your potential long before you did. I pushed you because I loved you fiercely. I pushed you because I believed what every good father believes:

"My children are capable of more than they think."

I never wanted easy lives for you. I wanted meaningful ones.

The Sky Is Not the Limit — It Is Only the Beginning

People will tell you the sky is the limit.

They are wrong.

The sky is simply the place where most people stop believing in themselves.

You — my children — were born to reach farther.

You were born with ambition stitched into your veins. With courage tucked into your heart. With the blood of generations who survived wars, droughts, depressions, and hardship flowing through you.

You come from endurance. From grit. From people who refused to quit even when quitting would have been easier.

When you stretch your hands toward your dreams, you carry them with you. When you rise, they rise again through you.

So do not shrink your dreams to make others comfortable. Do not extinguish your fire because others chose to live without theirs. Do not apologize for wanting a life larger than the one people expect from you.

Ambition is not arrogance.

Ambition is obedience to your calling.

And When You Fall — Because You Will — Remember This

You will stumble. You will fail. You will be misunderstood, underestimated, judged, and doubted.

You will face seasons of loneliness so heavy it feels like your lungs forget how to breathe.

And in those seasons, the world will not cheer for you.

Do not expect it to.

But do expect this:

You will rise. You will overcome. You will find your footing again.

You will discover depths of strength you never knew you carried. Failure was not your end. Failure was your beginning. Failure was the refinement that shaped you into the person you needed to become.

Family — Your First and Last Circle of Strength

There is something I want each of you to hold close to your heart:

Life is a path you must walk alone — but you were never meant to walk it without family.

Your siblings are not just playmates from childhood. They are the first friends God chose for you.

Your mother is not just the woman who raised you. She is the steady heart of this home.

And I… I am the imperfect man who will forever stand in your corner.

I will not always know the right answer. I will not always say the perfect thing. I will not shield you from every storm.

But I will always — always — believe in you.

Family is harbor and anchor. Family is quiet strength.

My Children — Chase Your Dreams Until Your Last Breath

Do not let fear write your future. Do not let comfort keep you small. Do not let the past chain you when God is calling you forward.

Jump when opportunity calls. Rise when life knocks you down. Grow when others choose to shrink.

Be brave enough to chase your ambitions… even if it means starting over.

Because one day, when I am old and gray, I will know you became everything I always believed you could be.

Letter 2 To My Children: Protect Your Name

My children,

One day — you will stand at the edge of adulthood and discover something quietly frightening.

The world does not know you. The world does not owe you. The world will not pause to wait for you.

On that day, when life feels too big and you feel impossibly small, you will search for something inside yourself to hold onto — something solid, something steady, something unshakable.

And that, my dear children, is where this letter begins.

Because you do have something. Something priceless. Something ancient. Something carved into the very bones of who you are.

You have a family name.

And a family name — if guarded faithfully — is worth more than riches, more than applause, more than titles, more than momentary glory.

A name is the one treasure you can carry from infancy to old age… the one treasure no one can take from you… the one treasure you will pass on long after I am gone.

Your name is your moral credit score — invisible, but powerful. Quiet, but unmistakable. Fragile, but enduring.

Protect it with everything you are.

The Weight of Those Who Carried It Before You

My children, you come from people who understood a simple truth:

A good name is built with calloused hands and tested hearts.

Both sides of your family — your mother's and mine — began on humble farm roads where no one waited for opportunity; they created it.

Your great-grandparents and their parents before them were not born into comfort. They were born into fields, into drought, into backbreaking work beneath the Texas sun.

They were born into a world where water was hauled, not delivered. Hay was cut by hand, not machine. Hands bled before dinner was served. Money stretched thin, but faith stretched further.

They were simple people by the world's standards — but giants by Heaven's.

They withstood the Great Depression not with bitterness, but with resolve. They went without so their children would not. They worked land that fought them. They carried burdens modern men would crumble beneath.

And still — they held their name with dignity.

When the world demanded even more — when war erupted across continents and oceans — your ancestors answered that call too.

Some crossed the mud-soaked battlefields of Europe. Some served across the vast Pacific, where the sea swallowed fear itself.

They endured hunger, cold, fire, and loss — not for medals, not for praise — but because their fathers taught them that a man stands between danger and the people he loves.

They fought because their name demanded courage.

And now that name rests in your hands.

The Name You Carry Is More Than Letters

One day, you will walk into a room filled with strangers — a job interview, a courtship dinner, a negotiation table — and before you ever say a word, your name will introduce you.

Your name will whisper who raised you. Your name will reveal what you value. Your name will carry the echo of every choice you've made. People won't remember your GPA. They won't remember your trophies. They won't remember the clothes you wore, the cars you drove, or the vacations you posted online.

But they will remember your name.

Your name can be a bridge or a barricade. A blessing or a burden. A lighthouse or a warning sign.

Tarnish it — even once — and you may spend years rebuilding what a moment destroyed. Honor it — and you will walk a path lit by trust.

Moral Choices: The Battle No One Sees

Life will tempt you — quietly, softly, persistently.

Rarely with loud sins, but with small compromises that feel harmless at first.

A tiny lie. A convenient omission. A shortcut justified by pressure. A selfish gain no one will ever know about.

But your soul knows. And your name remembers.

Understand this now while your hearts are still forming:

Your private choices will become your public reputation. Your invisible decisions will shape your visible future.

Choose honesty even when dishonesty would be easier. Choose truth even when truth has a cost. Choose humility over applause. Choose integrity over convenience. Choose the long road over the shortcut.

Your character is built in the silence — and revealed in the spotlight.

The Temptation to Betray Your Name

The world will promise you everything: Quick success. Easy wealth. Fast admiration. Instant validation.

But every shortcut demands payment — and many demand your character in return.

Guard your name from greed, jealousy, pride, and despair. Stand tall when others bend. Walk straight when others twist the truth. Rise when others hide behind excuses.

The strength of your name is the strength of your choices.

The Legacy You Inherit — and the Legacy You Will Leave

You bear a name carried across fields, wars, droughts, hardships, and quiet victories. You bear the prayers of your grandparents and their grandparents. You bear the sacrifices of men who fed cattle by lantern light and women who kept families standing when the world shook beneath them.

You are not the beginning of this story — but you are the next chapter.

One day you will realize this truth:

Legacy is not what you leave behind. Legacy is who you become while you are still here.

Your name will outlive you. Treat it as a gift. Treat it as a calling. Treat it as a responsibility worthy of your best.

Accountability — The Greatest Form of Love

You will be accountable for your actions. That is not punishment — that is love.

Hold yourself to a standard that honors your ancestors. Hold yourself to a standard that inspires your future children. Hold yourself to a standard that lets you sleep peacefully at night.

When you fail — and you will — own it quickly and correct it immediately.

A person who hides from their mistakes shrinks with every passing year. A person who learns from them grows into someone capable of leading others.

Mandino's Truth — and Your Father's Truth

Og Mandino wrote that a man is never truly defeated unless he stops trying.

I add this:

A man never truly rises unless he protects the name he carries.

You can lose your money. You can lose your job. You can lose comfort and opportunity.

But if you keep your name clean, you can rebuild anything.

What I Pray You Never Forget

Sometimes at dusk, when the sky softens into gold and the world quiets for a breath, I stand and think about who you will become.

And I whisper this prayer:

"Lord, let them carry our name with honor. Let them walk with humility. Let them choose integrity when no one is watching. Let them be brave when the world is loud. Let them be gentle when the world is harsh.

Let them rise after every fall. Let them be lights in dark places."

My children,

Protect your name. Honor your name. Strengthen your name.

And one day, pass it on shining.

Your legacy begins the moment you choose who you will be.

And I believe — with all that I am — that you will choose well.

Letter 3 To My Children: Ride for Your Brand

My children,

Every person ultimately rides for something.

Some ride for applause. Some ride for money. Some ride for comfort or convenience or whatever the world praises that day.

But the rarest among us — the ones who live with clarity and conviction — ride for something far deeper.

They ride for truth. They ride for purpose. They ride for a code that does not bend when pressure rises. They ride for a name worth honoring. They ride for a life worth building.

That is what I want to speak to you about now.

Not about accomplishments. Not about recognition. Not about anything the world would measure as success.

But about the truth that carried me from the ashes of starting over to the man I am today.

Your brand is not a logo. It is not a business. It is not a title. It is not a résumé line or a reputation you try to manage.

Your brand is the sum of who you choose to be when the world is watching and when it is not.

Ride for that. Guard that. Build that.

If you do, your life will take on a strength few ever find.

What It Means to "Ride for Your Brand"

This phrase — this guiding star of my life — does not come from a classroom or a business book.

It comes from the old ranching code, the unwritten law of the cattlemen and cowboys of Texas.

A man rode for the outfit he believed in. He worked with loyalty. He honored his commitments. He kept his word even when it cost him something. He took pride in the mark he represented.

But here is the deeper truth:

A good cowboy did not ride for the brand because he was told to. He rode for it because he believed in what it stood for.

He believed in the people. He believed in the work. He believed in the responsibility that came with carrying that mark.

One day, you will have to decide what you stand for.

Not what your friends value. Not what society praises. Not what seems easiest or most profitable. Not what earns quick applause.

But what is right. What is true. What aligns with the deepest part of your soul.

Whatever that is — ride for it with unwavering conviction.

The Brand You Carry Is Built in Ordinary Moments

You do not create your brand in a single heroic moment. You shape it quietly, steadily, in the thousand unseen decisions you make each day.

When you choose honesty over convenience, your brand strengthens.

When you return kindness for cruelty, your brand shines.

When you take responsibility instead of offering excuses, your brand grows.

When you refuse to betray your values, even when the world tempts you with something easier, your brand deepens.

Your brand will evolve. It will be tested. And yes, at times, you will fail.

Failure does not destroy a brand. Quitting on your principles does.

Choose your principles carefully. Protect them fiercely. Let them guide you when the road grows dark.

Ride for the Brand of Your Name

You come from generations who worked the land, who survived droughts, depressions, wars, and hardship not by luck, but by character.

They were not wealthy. They were not powerful. They were not celebrated.

But they carried something priceless: a reputation built on truth and a name carried with pride.

That is the brand you inherit.

Not money. Not land. Not comfort.

A legacy forged by sacrifice, preserved through humility, and carried with dignity.

Ride for that brand. Honor it. Strengthen it. Leave it better than you received it.

Your Brand Will Be Tested — That Is How It Is Forged

Life will not always be gentle with you.

Storms will come. Pressure will rise. The road will narrow.

The world will whisper lies into your heart: "That road is too hard." "No one believes in you." "You don't have what it takes." "Just quit." When those voices rise, remember this truth:

You build your brand by how you rise after you have been knocked to your knees.

Anyone can ride well in good weather.

But your true character — your true brand — is revealed when the trail turns steep, when the wind cuts cold, and when no one is clapping for you.

Hold steady. Stay true. Do not quit when you are tired — quit only when you are done.

Riding for Your Brand Means Serving Others

My greatest successes did not come from chasing titles, money, or recognition.

They came when I asked a simple question: "How can I serve someone today?"

Your brand becomes powerful the moment you realize it is not about you.

It is about lifting others. It is about honoring commitments. It is about giving more than you take. It is about telling the truth when lies would be easier. It is about choosing the harder right over the easier wrong.

A strong brand always reflects a strong heart.

Ride with Courage Into the Unknown

There will be seasons when everything familiar falls away.

Moments when you must start over. Moments when you must walk alone. Moments when the future feels foggy and uncertain.

Do not fear those moments.

Starting over is not a setback. It is a sacred invitation to rise higher.

You are my children — born with grit in your bones, faith in your blood, and the echoes of your ancestors in your spirit.

Ride boldly. Ride bravely. Ride like someone carrying a purpose larger than yourself.

Because you are.

What I Pray You Understand

Long after I am gone, long after my voice becomes a memory, long after I no longer stand in the soil of our hometown, I pray this truth remains:

You ride for your brand every single day of your life.

Not with horses. Not with cattle.

But with your choices, your character, your compassion, your courage.

Your brand is your legacy. Your brand is your truth. Your brand is the invisible mark others feel when your name is spoken.

So ride for your brand boldly. Ride for your brand humbly. Ride for your brand with a fire that does not fade.

And if you ever forget who you are, return to the values that built you and begin again.

For as long as I breathe, I will be proud of you.

And when my days are done, I pray the world sees in you the strength, the humility, and the heart I tried to live by.

Ride well, my children. Ride true. Ride for your name. Ride for your values. Ride for your purpose.

Ride for your brand.

Letter To My Future Generations

My dear ones — those who will carry our name long after my footsteps fade, those whose faces I may never see but whose lives I already pray for,

This letter is for you.

I write these words knowing full well that time will move on, that seasons will turn, and that the world you inherit will not be the world I walk today.

Technology will change. Customs will shift. Certainties I hold may no longer exist.

And yet, the truths that shaped me — the truths that shaped every generation before you — remain untouched by time.

I do not write to burden you with the weight of the past. I write to place a light in your hands — a light you may carry into whatever future awaits you.

So read these words slowly. Return to them when life grows heavy. For they are the sum of a lifetime of striving, stumbling, rising, and learning what truly matters.

I. You Come From People Who Endured — But You Were Born to Become

You do not need to memorize every name in our lineage nor carry the sorrow or hardship they endured.

What matters is this:

They endured so you would not have to. They sacrificed so you could reach higher. They walked so you could run.

They carried burdens you may never fully understand, and that is a gift.

But your destiny is not behind you — it is ahead.

Honor the past, but do not live in it.

You were not born merely to preserve what was. You were born to become what could be.

The world belongs to those who rise, who dare greatly, who love deeply, who walk with integrity even when the road grows dark.

My hope is not that you repeat our story, but that you continue it — with your own courage, your own brilliance, your own chapter worth passing forward.

II. The World Will Not Always Be Kind — So Be Kind Anyway

No matter the decade, no matter the country, no matter the culture — human beings will always wrestle with the same storms:

Jealousy. Fear. Doubt. Pride. And the temptation to choose the easy road over the right one.

You will be tested.

People may fail you. Friends may disappoint you. Opportunities may slip away. Plans may crumble.

And in the quiet hours of your hardest nights, you may question your worth.

Hear me clearly:

You are made for more than the storms that rise against you.

Be kind even when kindness feels foolish. Be honest even when honesty costs you something. Be faithful even when others abandon their posts.

And forgive — not because others deserve it, but because you deserve peace.

Kindness is never weakness. It is strength under control.

III. Your Life Is Yours — So Live It With Courage

There will be moments when you stand at a crossroads and feel utterly unprepared to choose.

Choose anyway.

There will be dreams that frighten you with their size and weight.

Chase them anyway.

You will feel unqualified, uncertain, or not enough.

Begin anyway.

Courage is not the absence of fear. It is choosing to move while fear begs you not to.

The greatest victories of your life will often be hidden behind one small act of bravery.

IV. Protect Your Name — And Live a Life Worth Signing

Every choice you make will sign your name on something:

Your reputation. Your relationships. Your future. Your legacy.

So choose well.

A good name will carry you into rooms your talents cannot open. It will preserve friendships, build trust, and shape how people remember you.

Protect your name — but more importantly, honor it.

Let your word mean something. Let your promises hold weight. Let your actions speak truths even your lips have not spoken.

And when you fall — for you will — rise with humility and repair what can be repaired.

There is no shame in falling. Only in refusing to rise.

V. Build a Life Rooted in Faith, Not Circumstance

Your world will offer quick fixes, shallow promises, and the illusion of easy success.

Resist it.

The foundation of your life must be something deeper, steadier, and greater than any earthly achievement.

Faith is not blind. Faith is seeing with the heart what your eyes cannot yet understand.

There will be seasons when you walk with no applause, no recognition, and no reassurance except the quiet whisper within:

"Do not stop. Better days are coming."

And they will come.

VI. Love Deeply — It Is the Only Treasure Time Cannot Steal

Love will cost you.

It will demand vulnerability, sacrifice, forgiveness, and courage.

But love — real love — is the only wealth that multiplies each time you give it away.

Cherish your family. Honor your parents. Protect your siblings. Stand together through storms.

Laugh loudly. Argue respectfully. Always come home with compassion.

Family is not perfect — but it is eternal.

VII. Ride for Your Brand — And Know What That Truly Means

This phrase will outlive me.

But I pray it does more than echo — I pray it guides you.

To ride for your brand means to live with loyalty, purpose, integrity, and clarity of identity.

Your brand is not a company. Not a title. Not a career.

Your brand is your soul.

It is the flame inside you that burns for something greater: Your values. Your faith. Your family. Your calling.

Ride for that. Protect that. Build your life around that.

When you know who you are, no storm can unmake you and no success can corrupt you.

VIII. My Hope for You — The Future I Pray You Walk Into

If time allows, perhaps one day you will sit where I sit now —
watching children laugh, watching seasons turn, watching life unfold
with wonder and humility.
And when you do, may you feel a quiet pride in knowing you lived
well, loved well, rose after every fall, and left the world better than you
found it.
I hope you chase dreams that set your soul on fire. I hope you build
something beautiful. I hope you find love that steadies you, faith that
anchors you, and purpose that calls you higher.
Above all, remember this:
You were never alone.
You carry the hopes of those before you and the promise of those
who will come after.
Walk wisely. Live boldly. Love deeply.
You are part of a legacy still being written. Write your chapter with
honor.
With all the love a man can give to those he may never meet but longs
to bless,
Steven Wiatrek

Conclusion: A Final Word to Those Walking Their Own Road

If these pages have taught you anything, I hope it is this:
You are allowed to begin again.
You are allowed to rebuild when life breaks you. You are allowed to rise when the ground beneath you gives way. And you are allowed to become someone your younger self never imagined possible.
That truth is not motivational. It is lived.
Everything I have written here is simply a witness to one reality I learned the hard way:
A man's life is not shaped by the moments that lift him, but by the moments that test him.
Those moments arrive without warning. They do not ask permission. And they do not care how prepared you feel.
They come as setbacks, failures, losses, and seasons of uncertainty that stretch longer than you expected. They come when plans fall apart, when trust is shaken, when confidence erodes quietly, day by day.
And when they come, you are faced with a choice.
Not a dramatic one. Not a public one. But a deeply personal one.
Will this moment define you — or refine you?
There is a lie we are often told — sometimes subtly, sometimes loudly — that strength means never falling.
That resilience means never breaking. That success means never starting over.
None of that is true.
Strength is not built in avoidance. Resilience is not forged in comfort. And success is rarely a straight line.

Most of the people you admire most are not impressive because of
what they achieved. They are impressive because of what they endured
and how they chose to respond.
Those people did not escape hardship. They walked through it.
And they came out clearer. Clearer about what matters. Clearer about
what doesn't. Clearer about who they are willing to become.
I am no different from you.
I am not stronger. I am not luckier. I am not chosen.
I am simply a man who refused to let the hardest season of his life
become the final chapter.
I doubted myself. I questioned my decisions. I wrestled with fear,
pride, anger, and uncertainty more than once.
There were moments when staying where I was would have been
easier. Moments when shrinking would have felt safer. Moments when
quitting would have spared me discomfort.
But ease has never built anything worth keeping.
So I chose to rebuild instead of retreat. To stand instead of disappear.
To grow instead of harden.
Not perfectly. Not without mistakes. But honestly.
That choice — repeated quietly over time — changed everything.
If there is anything I hope stays with you after the final page, it is this:
Your name is worth guarding. Your ambition is worth pursuing. Your
family is worth fighting for. Your faith is worth holding onto.
And your brand — your word, your integrity, your reputation — is
worth riding for with every breath God gives you.
You will be tempted to compromise. Not in obvious ways. But in
quiet decisions that seem harmless at first.
Those moments matter more than you realize. They are the moments
that shape who you become when no one is watching.
When your moment comes — when you find yourself standing at your
own crossroads, with fear on one side and possibility on the other —
may you choose courage.

Not loud courage. Not reckless courage.
But steady, grounded courage.
The kind that chooses forward even when the path is unclear. The kind that chooses integrity even when compromise is easier. The kind that chooses the long road when shortcuts whisper your name.
Because the world is not changed by the loudest voices.
It is changed by the quiet men and women who live with honor when no one is watching, who keep their promises long after the feeling fades, and who show up again and again even when the road feels lonely.
If this book has reached you, if a single sentence steadied your spirit, if one page gave you permission to keep going —
then every mile of the journey behind me was worth it.
Thank you for walking these pages with me.
And wherever life carries you next — go with courage, go with faith, go with your head high.
Protect what matters. Keep your word.
And above all — ride for your brand.

Closing Invitation

If this book has helped you in any way—whether it inspired you to pick up the phone, rebuild your confidence, or start fresh in your career—I'd love to hear from you.

Share your story. Tag me on LinkedIn:
(www.linkedin.com/in/steven-wiatrek-a96492125)

Let me celebrate your success right alongside you.

You never know who your story might inspire next.

And if you're willing, send me a picture and a short note about how this book made a difference in your career. Who knows—your story might be the one I share next to encourage another agent to keep going when times get tough.

Invite Steven Wiatrek to Speak

If this book inspired you or your team and you'd like me to share these lessons in person, I'd be honored to speak at your next event. Whether it's an agency meeting, corporate leadership retreat, or industry conference, I focus on helping agents reignite purpose, sharpen skills, and build businesses that last.

My sessions aren't lectures—they're conversations. Real stories. Real lessons. Real results. I teach from the same heart that built this book: practical, personal, and proven.

Topics Include:
- Purpose-driven sales and service
- Old-school fundamentals that still win
- Rebuilding after setbacks (resilience and leadership)
- Community, legacy, and client loyalty

Universities & Community Colleges
I speak at no charge for universities and community colleges—all I ask is that travel is covered and books are purchased for students.

Bookings & Bulk Orders
To discuss speaking opportunities, collaborations, or bulk book orders, contact me at:
LinkedIn: linkedin.com/in/steven-wiatrek-a96492125
Email: swiatrek@gmail.com

Let's continue building a stronger, more inspired community of agents—one meeting, one story, and one success at a time.

"A single voice can ignite a spark, but a united message can light the world."

www.ingramcontent.com/pod-product-compliance
Lightning Source LLC
Chambersburg PA
CBHW031038160726

47991CB00005B/1938